12-

GIRL IN A SLOPPY JOE SWEATER

GIRL IN A SLOPPY JOE SWEATER

Life On The Canadian Home Front During World War Two

By Mary Peate

Optimum Publishing International Inc.

Montreal Toronto

Published by Optimum Publishing International (1984) Inc., Montreal

© Ottawa 1988 Mary Peate

Legal deposit 3rd quarter 1989

National Library of Canada

Bibliothèque du Québec

Canadian Cataloguing in Publication Data

Peate, Mary, 1927-

Girl in a Sloppy Joe Sweater

ISBN 0-88890-222-0

1. Peate, Mary 1927- . 2. World War,

1939-1945 — Personal narratives, Canadian. 3. World War,

1939-1945 — Social aspects — Québec — Montréal. 4. Montréal

(Québec) — Social life and customs. I. Title.

PS8581.E39G57 1988   971.4'28103'0924   C88-090343-0

PR9199.3.P43G57 1988

Cover Illustration by Sharon Leggett

Printed and bound in Canada

For information, address:
Optimum Publishing International (1984) Inc.,
4255 Ste. Catherine W., Suite 100,
Montréal, Québec
H3Z 1P7

Michael S. Baxendale, President

CONTENTS

CHAPTER TITLE

Some of the characters in this book are composites. Many, but not all, of their names have been changed. Naming all of those with whom one has come in contact would be confusing to the reader, and serve no purpose.

Besides, as the Dickens character Sairey Gamp put it, "Which naming no names, no offense can be took."

There are many individuals and corporations to whom I am extremely grateful for permission to publish certain written and illustrative material included in this book.

My thanks to Kimberly-Clark Corporation, makers of KOTEX® and New Freedom® feminine care products, for permission to use its ARE YOU IN THE KNOW? advertisements from the 1940s. These wonderful ads were drawn by Irving Nurick and his illustration of the girl in a Sloppy Joe sweater appears on the front cover.

My gratitude to The Gazette of Montreal for their kind permission to use several newspaper clippings from the Montreal Star and The Gazette that appeared during the war years.

I am happy to be able to use the excerpt from the Screenplay of the Columbia Pictures Photoplay "Dead Reckoning", copyright 1947, renewed 1974 by Columbia Pictures Industries, Inc. All rights reserved.

Similar appreciation to the Meredith corporation for permission to repeat the "That's the Story" piece in Chapter 4 from Ladies' Home Journal, Felman 1947.

Thanks are also due to Smith-Corona, Cortland, NY, for authorizing me to reproduce one of their wartime typewriter advertisements; Stewart-Warner Corporation of Canada, Limited, of Belleville, Ontario; and Stewart-Warner Corporation 1826 West Diversey Parkway, Chicago, Illinois 60614, for consenting to my use of one of their wartime public service ads; to George Gobel for letting me quote one of his jokes as an epigraph; to Mr. and Mrs. Charles Brooks for placing that ad in The Westmount Examiner.

Finally my warmest thanks to my editor at Optimum Publishing, Laurel Sullivan, for her helpful suggestions and for keeping my manuscript lean and trim.

This book is lovingly dedicated to Bob and all the people who are the result of the meeting of the jitterbug and the drummer that New Year's Eve — George, Rick, Candy, and Danny, Mary Clare, Joey, and Johnny.

— and to all the girls who wore Sloppy Joe sweaters

"Say, when you get on again as a professor at some college, and I'm back running my cabs in St. Louis, ... send me up a (girl) in a Sloppy Joe sweater."

> — Humphrey Bogart to Army
> buddy in World War Two
> film "Dead Reckoning"

"I was a fighter pilot during the war. You remember the war; it was in all the papers."

> — George Gobel

PROLOGUE

Over the years, whenever my husband referred to his days as a pilot in the RCAF during the Second World War, one of our children would inevitably ask, "What did *you* do in the war, Mom?" and I would quote Milton defensively, "They also serve who only stand and wait."

Had they asked if I wore a uniform while I was in this "service", I would have said, "Yes, I did — in a way: — a Sloppy Joe sweater, pearls, skirt, bobbysocks and saddleshoes."

And had they asked, "Was war hell, Mom?" I would have had to admit, "Not hell exactly, but you could say that on the homefront 'War is heck'."

CHAPTER ONE

"C'EST LA GUERRE"

"My mother's going back to church this aft' to pray for peace," Cath said, as we walked home from Mass that Sunday of Labor Day weekend, 1939.

"She is?" I asked. Jeepers, imagine going to church twice in one day when you didn't have to. But then Cath's mother was very religious. You could tell, because she always called Jesuits "Jebbies".

That kind of familiarity suggested a more inside position with the church than my mother had.

Cath's parents often had priests come to dinner, sometimes as weekend guests. The only time we had a priest in our house was when one of the parish priests made an annual visit.

Even her mother's conversation was sprinkled with prayers: like one day she said to Cath, "Glory be to God, I'm out of soap. Will ya run up to the A & P for some P & G?"

Another time, when she offered me a plate of temptingly decorated cookies, I did what the nuns had taught us to do, chose the least interesting one on the plate, and she said, "Jesus, Mary, and Joseph, will ya look at the poor plain orphan of a cookie she took."

Still, even though Cath's mother was religious, there were incon-sistencies in her thinking. For instance, she wouldn't let Cath invite a certain girl to one of her birthday parties because the girl was Italian. Yet she had a picture of Pope Pious XII over her bed. And he was Italian.

My mother was also inconsistent. For some reason, though her own father and my father had been Protestants, and she loved them both dear-ly, she always lowered her voice when she said the word "Protestant".

And though she was religious, Cath's mother said, "My God!" a lot.

My mother said, "My word!"

Cath's mother baked airy little biscuits she called "Nun's farts."

My mother would never say such a thing.

My mother would never believe a nun would *do* such a thing.

My mother and Cath's mother also reacted differently to electrical storms. If there was thunder and lightning, my mother would say, "It's a kind of a day for reading Emily Bronte." (Just as when there was a soft spring rain she would say it was "the kind of a day for reading Jane Aus-ten.")

But when I was at Cath's place during a storm, her mother sprinkled us with holy water and made us take the metal barrettes out of our hair lest we be conductors of electricity. Then she would make a sign of the Cross and pray that we'd come through the thunder and lightning safe-ly. And we did. So there was no reason for me to be surprised that she would be praying for peace, except that I couldn't see the point of it since Britain had declared war on Germany early that morning.

"You're lucky your brother is just a little kid," I told Cath, "If Canada gets in the war, he won't have to go."

"I know," Cath agreed, "When we heard the news on the radio this morning, the first thing my mother said was, "Blessed be the great mother of God, Bertie's too young to go," Cath imitated her mother's brogue, then went on, "I wonder what it will be like if Canada *does* go to war."

I was wondering the same thing. On this clear, balmy Labor Day weekend, with the temperature around 80 degrees, and the beginning scents of autumn in the air, N.D.G. had never looked more peaceful.

Notre Dame de Grace, the Montreal neighborhood we lived in, was primarily Irish, with residents with names like the woodwind section of MacNamara's band. There were Hennesseys and Hanrahans, and Hef-fernans, and though I wasn't Irish myself, most of my classmates were .

Cath and I were to start the 6th grade the following day. We had gone to the same school since Preparatory Class (the one before 1st grade) but it wasn't until she moved to my street the year before that we had become best friends. By coincidence, she had moved into the flat vacated when my friend Margaret moved back to Halifax.

Out of the blue, as we approached our street, a thought struck me. A ray of light in all the gloom. I turned to her, excited, "If Canada goes to war, we won't have to go to school!"

"Who said?" she asked, looking skeptical.

"Nobody said, but figure it out. Kids would have to be at home in case anything happened."

"Like what?"

"Like if Montreal gets bombed."

"Gee, do you think Montreal will get bombed?"

"Who knows? Could be. And if it does, think of all the mixups and everything if kids were in school. I bet they'll announce it on the radio."

As I walked into our flat, I could hear the radio giving the latest bulletins, and cocked an ear for the announcement that the schools would remain closed, but school was never mentioned.

At lunchtime, our family gathered in the dining-room, where our radio was located, to half-heartedly eat lunch as we listened to the King speak.

"In this grave hour," he began, "perhaps the most fateful in our history, I send to every household of my peoples, both at home and overseas, this message, spoken with the same depth of feeling for each of you as if I were able to cross your threshold and speak to you myself."

King George VI *had*, in effect, "crossed our thresholds" just a few months before, when he toured Canada with his Queen, in May of 1939. As Girl Guides, Cath and I proudly stood in the Guard of Honor on Shakespeare Road (later to be renamed Remembrance Road in honor of the occasion), and watched enthralled, as they drove by in an open car, the Queen gently waving, and smiling her sweet smile, just a few feet away from where we stood. She seemed to be surrounded by an aura of graciousness. We were absolutely captivated by her, and fell madly in love with our handsome King. Never mind that he had two daughters back in England close to our age. We filled thick scrapbooks with pictures and newspaper clippings of the visit.

My mother dabbed at her eyes with a handkerchief as he asked us to "stand calm and firm and united in this time of trial". Then she reached over to my brothers, Choate and Bill, and held on to their wrists.

"What do you think, Dad?" Choate, the older of the two, asked. "Will we be in it too?"

15

My father was considered the authority on such matters. Because he was an artist at *The Montreal Star*, we all believed he had the inside dope on world events.

"There's no question about it," my father answered, and my mother tightened her grip on my brothers' wrists. I felt a lump form in my stomach.

"Do you think Choate will have to go to war?" I asked my mother. Choate was my favorite. He turned to me now with a jaunty grin. "I might have to go away to help keep Canada out of Hitler's clutches, but it won't be for a while, shrimp." He was the only one who called me that. I'd miss him if he went. He always kept our mealtimes lively. He could imitate Ben Bernie — "This is the Old Maestro, Ben Bernie, bidding you cheerio, a bit of a pip-pip, tweet-tweet, and au revoir, yowsah, yowsah, yowsah." He could hold up a wire coat hanger in one hand and spin a dime on it with the other; and sometimes he'd get up from the table when dinner was over, and tap dance — just for the heck of it.

If Choate went to war, I thought he might come back with a leg or arm missing. The man who lived across the street from us had lost an arm in the previous war.

"I thought you said the last war was called 'the war to end all wars'," I said to my father.

"Yes. That was a laugh," he said, not laughing. "I'm going to give The Star a call," he said, getting up, and the family dispersed — my mother and Helena, my older sister, to the kitchen to make a pot of tea, and my brothers to their room. As my father dialed The Star I went out to sit on the front steps to sort it all out.

For some time now my father had been bringing art work home to do at night. After my mother and Helena did the dishes, he set out his work on the kitchen table, first putting out a wooden drawing board; thumb-tacking a sheet of white posterboard to it; then dipping a fine-nibbed pen into a white porcelain container of black ink, and drawing in minute detail, a new map of Europe each time Adolf Hitler took over another country.

Sometimes I sat opposite him and worked on my stamp collection as he drew. My orders were not to jiggle the table under penalty of death. Once he looked over at the stamps I was attaching hinges to and said, "Better not trade any of your Danzig stamps."

"How come?" I asked. Cath and I often traded duplicates.

"Because it won't be long before there won't be a place by that name."

16

And now Hitler had taken over Danzig.

My father had been right about that, so I guessed he'd probably be right about Canada going to war. I went back inside to listen to the radio.

I'd always hated Labor Day weekend anyway, because it signalled so definitely the end of summer vacation, but this Labor Day weekend of 1939 would go down as the worst.

The bulletins I heard reiterated British Prime Minister Neville Chamberlin's declaration of war early that morning; quoted excerpts of the King's speech, as well as Canadian Prime Minister Mackenzie King's message, but nowhere was there any news of the schools remaining closed.

It made no sense to me that the schools should open just because Canada had not yet declared herself. I wanted to caution restraint on the part of the school boards. Why be hasty? Why not wait a while and see? What was the point in opening the schools only to have to close them again in a day or two?

The next day, Labor Day, there was another big news event.

When I went out to the front steps to pick up *The Gazette*, I saw that the headline read: ATHENIA TORPEDOED WITH 1,400 PASSENGERS: SHIP BOUND HERE SUNK OFF SCOTTISH COAST.

When I handed the paper to my mother, she said, "Quick, go turn on the radio." Gosh, what an exciting world we were living in. Is this how it would be from now on?

Later in the day, Cath and I were leaning over the dining-room table reading the passenger list, to see if there were any familiar names on board.

"There," Cath said, pointing to a name, "Miss Margaret Patch, daughter of Howard H. Patch, jeweller. My mother goes to that jewellery store."

"Oh, sure."

"She *does*. When my cousin Myrna got married, she bought her gift there."

I scanned the list.

"I know them," I said, pointing to the names of Judith Evelyn, a Toronto actress, and Andrew Allen, a Toronto radio announcer.

"You do not."

"Well I may not know them personally, but I heard them on the radio."

"When?"

"When I went to Toronto with my mother to visit my aunt," I improvised.

"I'll bet," she sniffed.

The conversation reminded me of when I'd started reading the birth columns in the newspaper. I was pleasantly interested to see someone I knew had had a baby — the mother of someone in my class at school perhaps, like Mrs. O'Brien, who had a baby girl every year for five years in a row, just like clockwork. But as my eye travelled from the birth to the obituary column, I found myself still pleasantly interested in seeing a familiar name. I'd see a surname like Jones, for instance, and think, oh, I know a Jones, then scan the notice eagerly for the words "survived by", and read all the names, looking for the name of the person I knew. When I didn't see it, I'd feel a momentary stab of disappointment. When I realized how anxious I was to see a familiar name in the paper, I stopped reading the obituary columns altogether. I stopped reading the Athenia passenger list for the same reason.

Again the radio was on all day, and I continued to listen for the announcement that the schools would remain closed, but no such luck. The next day school opened right on schedule.

Parliament met on the 7th, and while it was debating whether Canada should go to Britain's aid, another event occurred that (dare I say it?) interested us more than what was going on in Parliament. Gloria Jean, the new singing child star, made a personal appearance at the Capitol Theatre in downtown Montreal, in connection with the opening of her first picture, "The Underpup".

We were interested in her because as far as we knew, she was the first child star to make a personal appearance in Montreal. And I was interested because not only were Gloria Jean and I around the same age, but I closely resembled her. Gloria Jean herself looked like Deanna Durbin, and was being groomed by her discoverer, Joseph Pasternak (who had also discovered Deanna Durbin) for roles that Deanna Durbin had grown too old to play. The reason I looked like Gloria Jean was that I was trying to look like Deanna Durbin, by wearing my hair in the same length and style as she. Deanna Durbin, a native of Winnipeg, Manitoba, was the role model for most North American girls.

"The Underpup" was about a slum girl who wins a school essay contest and gets to spend the summer at an exclusive girls' camp. Her winning essay was about her never having seen a tree. Cath and I had no trouble buying a premise like that.

18

Universal's promotion department had made a serious error by including Montreal on Gloria Jean's itinerary because Montreal had a law prohibiting children under 16 admittance to movie theatres. As a result the very audience they hoped to attract, would be excluded.

"They're mean not letting kids in to see it," I said to Cath. "I bet if I went, and Joseph Pasternak saw me in the audience, he'd see how much I look like Gloria Jean and hire me as her stand-in."

"What makes you think *he'll* be there?"

"He's the one who discovered her. Of course he'll be there," I said. Cath wasn't as wise in the ways of Hollywood as I.

"Anyway it said in the paper that Gloria Jean's *sister* is her stand-in," Cath said.

So much for fame and fortune.

Gloria Jean's movie opened at the Capitol on the same day as "The Wizard of Oz" at Loew's in downtown Montreal. Wonder of wonders, Montreal's movie law was relaxed enough for that one movie so that children were allowed to see it if accompanied by an adult. Perhaps the concession was made because the film was billed as "A Picture To Make The World Forget Its Troubles", and would boost morale. The number one song on the Hit Parade that week was one from that movie, and promised that our troubles could melt like lemon drops somewhere "Over The Rainbow".

In the issue that announced the arrival of Gloria Jean and "The Wizard Of Oz", *The Montreal Star* published the latest map of Europe that my father had drawn, suggesting that its readers clip it out and consult it in the days ahead, which of course I did, since it was my father's work, and tacked it to the back of my bedroom door.

On Sunday, September 10th, Canada was officially at war with Germany.

The next morning, I was in uniform. My school uniform. I had been all wrong. War or no war, kids still had to go to school.

While the Canadian Army uniform consisted of high waisted trousers with a big pocket on one leg and a blouse-like tunic also sporting large pockets; our school uniform was a scratchy navy blue serge dress with starched white collar and cuffs.

Not only was it uncomfortable; it lacked style. Mother Superior had seen to that. Upppermost in her mind was that it be of modest design. Accordingly, it had side pleats that ran from shoulder to hem, to make you look flat-chested for as long as possible — preferably until after graduation. If your breasts started to develop, the blossoming was hid-

19

den by the pleats, tucks, and gussets on either side of the bodice so that you stuck out a little further, but not provocatively, mind. A girl at my parochial school could come into the full flower of young womanhood without anyone knowing, or indeed, caring.

Within the first few days of war being declared, hundreds of Canadian girls and women flocked to the Red Cross volunteer offices to offer their services as nurses and ambulance drivers. Stories illustrating the British stiff upper lip began appearing in the newspapers, such as the church bulletin board bearing the legend: IF YOUR KNEES KNOCK, KNEEL ON THEM; and a picture of Queen Elizabeth with a gas mask jauntily draped over her arm, just like any common lass.

Canadian public school kids, wearing Red Cross lapel buttons, collected money for the Red Cross by going door to door selling Red Cross calendars. Catholic school kids didn't collect for the Red Cross, (perhaps because we were too busy collecting for the pagan Chinese babies) but we offered up a prayer every day for the allies.

Junior I.O.D.E. (Imperial Order Daughters Of The Empire) members knitted garments for overseas babies and servicemen, as did the Canadian Girls In Training, and the Girl Guides. Others sorted clothing donated for Overseas Bundles, or found a variety of ways of raising money for the Red Cross, such as having toy, bake, and rummage sales.

Just as there was school as usual even though there was a war in progress, so too were all the rituals and rites of holidays observed.

Registration Days at McGill University took place as always at the end of September. At the end of October, after it had been suggested that McGill's Junior Prom be cancelled on account of the war, it was decided to hold it anyway, and to hand over the proceeds to the Canadian Red Cross.

The late fall production of Dorothy Davis and Violet Walters' Children's Theatre proceeded on schedule at Victoria Hall; Hallowe'en saw the usual dressing up and handouts of candy; and Christmas traditions prevailed. Kids still visited Santa Claus in Eaton's Department Store's Toyville; rode the Toyville train; and were treated to lunch in the Art Deco purity of Eaton's ninth floor restaurant.

There was one difference in that first Christmas of war. It was in some of the Christmas gift items being advertised. Suggested gifts for the armed forces were money belts, roll-up kits for toilet articles, and sterling silver identification bracelets.

One entrepreneur introduced a board game called "Blackout", the object of which was to blackout your city. Further evidence of the preoccupation with blackouts was the new dance in Britain called The Black-out Stroll, which promised to rival in popularity its predecessor, The Lambeth Walk.

On December 19th, when I went out to pick up the cold Gazette from the doorstep, I experienced my first rush of patriotic pride, the kind that brings color to your cheeks and moisture to your eyes. There was a picture of the Royal Montreal Regiment on the front page. The story said that the first contingent of the Canadian Active Service Force had landed in England to British cheers of welcome.

In the scant three months since the war had begun, these 20,000 Canadian men had been trained and had now arrived in Great Britain. When I read how glad the British were to see them, and how dramatic their arrival had been, I felt another surge of pride.

No one knew they were coming. The people in the port town were just going about their business, attending church on Sunday morning, when out of the mist appeared this convoy of ships, coming to their aid. What a moment it must have been. Winston Churchill, First Lord of the Admiralty, was so happy, he announced the great news 27 hours ahead of the time he'd agreed upon. For the British people it must have seemed as if Christmas had come early, and 20,000 Santas dressed in khaki had arrived in steel grey ships instead of sleighs.

On Christmas morning, as I sat on the floor opening my presents, I listened to the King deliver his annual Christmas message. Those trans-atlantic speeches always had a sound in the background that I identified as the pounding of the ocean waves. The King's voice ebbed and swelled like the tide, first soft, then louder as he quoted:

"I said to a man who stood at the gate of the year, 'Give me a light that I may tread safely into the unknown,' and he replied, 'Go out into the darkness and put your hand into the hand of God. That shall be to you better than light and safer than the known way'."

He ended his message with the words, "May that Almighty hand guide and uphold us all."

It was a good invocation for the coming year of our Lord, nineteen hundred and forty.

THE KING'S MESSAGE

London, September 3.—(A.P.)—The text of the address of the King to his subjects in all parts of the world today follows:

In this grave hour, perhaps the most fateful in our history, I send to every household of my peoples, both at home and overseas, this message, spoken with the same depth of feeling for each one of you as if I were able to cross your threshold and speak to you myself.

For the second time in the lives of most of us, we are at war.

Over and over again, we have tried to find a peaceful way out of the differences between ourselvs and those who are now our enemies; but it has been in vain.

We have been forced into a conflict, for we are called, with our allies, to meet the challenge of a principle which, if it were to prevail, would be fatal to any civilized order in the world.

It is a principle which permits a state in the selfish pursuit of power to disregard its treaties and its solemn pledges, which sanctions the use of force or threat of force against the sovereignty and indeperdence of other states.

Such a principle, stripped of all disguise, is surely the mere primitive doctrine that might is right, and if this principle were established through the world, the freedom of our own country and of the whole British Commonwealth of nations would be in danger.

But far more than this, the peoples of the world would be kept in the bondage of fear, and all hopes of settled peace and of security, of justice and liberty, among nations, would be ended.

This is the ultimate issue which confronts us. For the sake of all that we ourselves hold dear, and of the world order and peace, it is unthinkable that we should refuse to meet the challenge.

It is to this high purpose that I now call my people at home and my peoples across the seas who will make our cause their own.

I ask them to stand calm and firm and united in this time of trial.

The task will be hard. There may be dark days ahead, and war can no longer be confined to the battlefield, but we can only do the right as we see the right, and reverently commit our cause to God. If one and all we keep resolutely faithful to it, ready for whatever service or sacrifice it may demand, then with God's help, we shall prevail.

May He bless and keep us all.

CHAPTER TWO

FOREIGN CORRESPONDENT

Cath and I regarded the new law in August of 1940 as a personal affront: All Canadian residents, 16 and over, were obliged to register.

"Now we'll *never* be able to get into a movie," Cath complained.

I couldn't argue with her. Owning a Registration Card was proof positive that you were 16, and legitimately eligible to get into Montreal's movie theatres. If you didn't have a card, there was no use in pleading looking young for your age to the cashier; she just turned you away.

Lucky for me, on Labor Day weekend that year, when the war was a year old, my mother took me to Toronto to visit her sister. While we were there, they took me to a movie called "Foreign Correspondent" starring Joel McCrea as Johnny Jones, the foreign correspondent. Watching him in the final scene, broadcasting from London during an air raid, while outside, bombs were falling, sirens wailing, and "America" was playing on the soundtrack, I knew I had a new goal to work toward.

On the day after Labor Day, as we walked to school together, I told Cath about the movie. I probably didn't outline very clearly the convoluted plot involving kidnapping, drugging, doubles, double agents, and Nazis, because as I described it to her, her eyes seemed to glaze over.

"What exactly *is* a foreign correspondent, anyway?" she asked irritably.

"It's a reporter who goes all over the world and sends back stories to the newspaper or radio station he works for, and guess what? It's what I'm going to be when I grow up."

"You *are*?"

"Yes, but I'll probably have to change my name to something more interesting than Mary Todd. Johnny Jones, the foreign correspondent in the movie, had to change his name to Huntley Haverstock. They told him that Johnny Jones didn't sound ritzy enough for a foreign correspondent. I was thinking maybe Priscilla Pomrose would be good. Or Pomfret. It doesn't really matter right now anyway. I don't have to decide right away."

I liked the other reporter in the movie too. He was played by George Sanders, an actor with a lovely British accent who described his job as a reporter as "doing a bit of noticing" — one of those British understatements that say so much more than American overstatements. Much was made of his name in the film too, and its spelling. It was Herbert Ffolliott. Maybe I could spell mine Priscilla Ppomffrett.

"I don't think ladies are allowed to be foreign correspondents," Cath broke into my thoughts.

"Why not?"

"Because they get their monthlies."

"*What*?"

"You know, the curse."

"Well what's *that* got to do with the price of eggs?"

"Because, *you* know, they get cramps. And you can't travel all over the world where wars and things are going on if you've got the curse. My mother says you can't even wash your hair then. She knows of someone who got a permanent when she had the curse, and died. Besides, being a foreign correspondent would be too dangerous for a lady."

I decided to check out Cath's theory with my father — not the part about the curse, but about the danger.

Whenever I wanted to have a conversation with him, I had two times in the day to catch him. One was just as he came home from work, and the other was at the dinner table. At all other times he was sitting in the living-room, reading.

Once he'd settled down for the evening to read, if there was something I wanted to ask or tell him, as he raised his head to listen or answer, he put a finger on the word he'd just left off reading, so as not to miss a moment's reading when our conversation was through.

A childhood accident had left him lame, and a line in Jane Austen's *Persuasion* fitted him perfectly: "His lameness prevented his taking much exercise; but a mind of usefulness and ingenuity seemed to furnish him with constant employment within."

That evening I sat down on the sofa opposite his chair and said, "Dad, Cath says women can't be foreign correspondents because it's too dangerous. Do you think that's true?"

He looked up, taking a second to come back to the living-room from wherever his book had taken him. "Nonsense," he said, "women have been foreign correspondents for years — all the way back to Margaret Fuller, who lived in the same town as Emerson and Thoreau, and at the same time."

Emerson and Thoreau's names cropped up often in his conversation. When I was younger, I had thought they were friends of his; he spoke of them with such frequency and familiarity. One summer he had taken the train from our favorite vacation spot in Maine to Concord, Massachusetts, to see their homes, walk in their woods, and sit by their pond. I wished he'd taken me, because he told me that he had seen Orchard House where Louisa May Alcott lived when she wrote *Little Women*. She had known Emerson and Thoreau too.

"Margaret Fuller was the first U.S. woman journalist," he went on. "She was writing for the *New York Tribune* when her boss, Horace Greeley, the same chap who said "Go west, young man", sent her to Europe. That made her the first female foreign correspondent. She was there during the Roman Revolution in the mid-1880s, and she covered that, so that made her the first woman war correspondent. And of course you've heard of Nellie Bly." I hadn't. "Well she went around the world in —" He laid the book he'd been reading out flat, and reached for the first book of an encyclopedia in the book rack table beside his chair. Oh gosh, he's going to look it up, I thought, almost regretting my question. I might be going to hear more about foreign correspondents than I wanted to know.

Once, when I'd asked him about how newspapers were printed, he described every step of the process from how pulpwood is made into newsprint, to how the linotype machine was operated. And for good measure, he threw in the story of how, when the English statesman, Edmund Burke, was delivering a speech in the British House of Commons in the 1700s, at the time when European society was thought of as being divided into Three Estates, (the Clergy, the Nobility, and the Commons), Burke pointed to the Reporters' Gallery and said, "Yonder sits the Fourth Estate, more important far than them all." When I heard that, I felt a shiver run between my shoulder blades, and it was at that moment that I resolved to become a newspaper reporter when I grew up.

My father stopped at a page in the enclycopedia and said, "Nellie Bly went around the world in 1889, while working for Joseph Pulitzer's World. She made the trip by train, boat, burro, barouche, rickshaw, and sampan, freezing and roasting, and she did it all in 72 days. That beats Phileas Fogg by a country kilometer."

Whoever Phileas Fogg was. He often assumed that I had heard of all the people he had. I didn't like to remind him that since he had been fifty when I was born, there were probably quite a few people he knew about that I didn't.

Putting the book back, he said, "Then there was Elinor Glyn, who was a war correspondent during the last world war."

"Aren't there any women foreign correspondents now?" I asked, "Those people all lived in the olden days."

"Of course there are. There's Dorothy Thompson, for one. She's a foreign correspondent who travels all over the world for *The New York Herald Tribune*. She's married to Sinclair Lewis. And she's good, too. So tell Cath to put *that* in her pipe and smoke it." I didn't dare ask who Sinclair Lewis was.

His saying that Dorothy Thompson was good was quite an admission, coming from him. He generally never read a book written by a woman if he could help it. Some women used men's names or just their initials in their names (probably because they were aware of such prejudices) and that would fool him sometimes. Mrs. Wand, the librarian at the lending library on Sherbrooke Street near Marcil Park, knowing how he felt, often put one over on him by giving him one of their books. I knew, because it was my job to go to the library to pick up and return his books and report his reaction to them. Based on these reports and the fact that he had borrowed there for so long, she knew his reading tastes well. Something else that guided her was his habit, if he really enjoyed a book, of penciling his initials, V.E.T., in the back of it. Many other readers, she told me, looked at the back of books to see if his initials were there, because it generally followed that if he liked a book, they would too.

His feeling the way he did about women writers hadn't deterred me from deciding at age nine that I was going to be a writer. Though I had

26

been going to be a newspaper reporter, I now had a more clearly defined goal.

I would wear one of those trench coats with gun flaps, cuff straps, D-rings, storm pockets, epaulets, and cape shoulders like the one Joel McCrea wore in "Foreign Correspondent", and I'd tie the belt as he did, instead of buckling it. I would carry a portable typewriter, and roam the world, wherever news was being made, and however noisily.

"Do you think when I'm old enough, I'll be able to report on this war?" I asked my father.

"I certainly hope not. It had better be over long before then. I tell you what you *could* do, though. You could keep track of what's happening here, on this side of the ocean. On the home front. We're doing something like that at The Star. We're putting out a newspaper called *The Home-Front News* for Star employees in uniform. You could keep a scrapbook, or journal, or diary, or whatever, of all the things that are going on here, while the war is on. I've often wished I'd done that during the last war — kept clippings and made notes of all the day-to-day developments. It would be interesting to read now. And since you want to be a writer anyway, it would be good practice for you."

"You mean a scrap book like the one I kept on the Royal visit?"

"Something like that, yes."

It sounded like a good idea to me. That evening I went through a stack of papers that my mother had been saving because they contained art work done by my father, and clipped out anything that seemed to be relevant or worth keeping, and, at my father's suggestion, for my first page, I used the logo from The Star's *The Home-Front News*.

Canadian Troops in U.K. Lonely
Despite Hospitality of English

Aldershot, England, December 25. —(?)—Christmas came today to Canada's men in khaki with the warmth of a full-hearted English welcome to the visitor far from home. But even the friendly brandy flaming on plum pudding did not dispel a touch of loneliness for the folks left behind.

Hospitable suburbanites showered the Canadian Active Service Force with invitations assuring a Christmas dinner in an English home for everyone desiring it. More than 1,000 were on leave with friends or relatives. Special provision was made for the troops in such London places as the Victoria League Club where a comfortable bed and breakfast for a five-day leave totals 10 shillings. All Christmas Day meals were free.

Thousands remaining in camp joined the morning church services which were exceptionally well attended. All chaplains stressed the appreciation felt by Canadians over the welcome extended to the troops, adding that naturally, home being the centre of the Christmas celebration, the troops' thoughts were directed toward Canada.

One chaplain expressed the feeling in this way: "Some of the boys are a bit lonely despite the kindness of the English people and the fact many comrades were granted leave together. Young lads away from home for the first time, and fathers separated from their families, can not prevent the suggestion of a tear in the eye. Delay of letters and parcels in the mail does not help. However all realize that everything possible has been done to make them happy."

Dinner was held at noon in the various messes, decorated with holly, where the chill, foggy weather outside was forgotten. There was fun aplenty in the afternoon's special Christmas program which was broadcast to Canada.

The boys apparently were thrilled to realize that a mass message had been transmitted home.

Everybody turned in early, because of the dampening blackout and in preparation for the Boxing Day program when Brigadier G. R. Pearkes, V.C., Commander of the Second Infantry Brigade, will take the salute at the march past.

"Girls Left Behind"

First-of-Its-Kind
Club In Dominion
Has 16 Members

FREDERICTON, Dec. 20 — (B.U.P.) — Believed to be the first of its kind in the Dominion, the "girls left behind club" has been organized here to help wives, mothers and sisters of men on active service to overcome their loneliness. Formality is taboo at its meetings, and membership is free—provided the would-be member has a loved one on active service. The club, with an initial membership of 16, plans a program of war service.

CHAPTER THREE

THE BRITISH (KIDS) ARE COMING

Canada began admitting its first war refugee children in July and August of 1940, in time to start school. Two of them were in our class that September. They were sisters, one red-headed, with orange freckles and a gritty voice, and the other, dark-haired and quiet.

It wasn't long before it became evident to everyone in the class that they were ahead of us academically. They had already started on Dickens and Shakespeare at school in England, whereas we had not yet dealt with either. Had it not been for my mother having read Dickens aloud to me, and my father quoting Shakespeare whenever apropos, I would have been even more put off by their erudition. Their precociousness immediately earned them teacher's pet status, along with their situation, which probably stirred sympathetic feelings in our teacher's breast.

Though we had no school library, I had always borrowed books from everyone I knew, and had considered myself the best-read member of any class I'd been in. Now it looked as if my position were being usurped. I immediately cast myself in competition with them, showing off my literary knowledge whenever I could. Every conversation we had together took the form of a contest.

After a series of confrontations, it was established that they had never read *Anne of Green Gables, Little Women, Tom Sawyer, Huckleberry Finn*, and *A Girl of The Limberlost*; I had never read *The Secret Garden, The Wind In The Willows, Hans Brinker, Or The Silver Skates, Peter Pan, Gulliver's Travels, Lad, A Dog*, and *The Water-Babies*; but we had all read *Heidi* and *Black Beauty*.

They had never heard of the book that bore my favorite title, *And To Think That It Happened On Mulberry Street*; and though I hadn't read *A Little Princess*, I had seen the movie version of it with Shirley Temple as Sarah Crewe. Likewise, though I hadn't read *Alice In Wonderland*, I had been Tweedledee in *Through The Looking Glass*, our school play of the previous year.

"Have you read any of Maysie Greig's books?" I asked them.

They hadn't.

"You come from England and you haven't read any books by Maysie Greig? They take *place* in England!" And these girls called themselves readers! The dark one shrugged, and looked pained.

"Have you read any books by Angela Brazil?" she asked.

"I bet I've read them all," I bragged. "Did you go to a boarding school like the ones she writes about?"

"No, we lived at home," said the older girl.

"Have you read *Winnie The Pooh*?" the younger one wanted to know. "Yes," I said, then made haste to add, "A long time ago."

"Do you have it?" she asked.

"No. I borrowed it from a girl named Marylou who used to go to this school."

"Could you borrow it from her again?"

"No. She boards at Villa Marie convent now. Her mother works, and Marylou only comes home on week-ends."

"Could you borrow it from her at week-end?" She pronounced it week *end*.

"No."

"Why not?"

"Because. If I phone her and ask her for it, if her mother answers the phone she'll ask me to Sunday dinner."

"What would be wrong with that?"

"I don't want to go there for Sunday dinner, that's all."

"Why?"

"Because," I was getting irritated, "I don't like Marylou that much."

Unaccountably, the redhead began to cry.

I looked at the dark-haired girl.

"Mummy used to read us *Winnie The Pooh*," she said quietly, by way of explanation.

I didn't know what to say to that. It was just that I didn't want to start with Marylou. She had never been a close friend, but when she was in my class I had availed myself of the contents of her bookshelves. She was an only child, and had a good sized library.

Her mother, however, had the mistaken notion that we were bosom buddies. Every time I saw her on Sherbrooke Street she invited me to Sunday dinner. I didn't feel like going through all that just to borrow a copy of *Winnie The Pooh*, which was a baby book anyway; and I wasn't particularly anxious to look at the fact that the only reason I had been friendly with Marylou was so that I could borrow her books.

"There aren't any children's libraries in N.D.G., but Westmount Library has a children's section. Do you know where it is?" I asked.

They shook their heads.

"I could show you," I said. "You couldn't take the books out, but you could read them there."

They looked at each other. "Want to have a go?" the older one asked her sister, and the younger one nodded.

So we made arrangements to meet in the school yard on the following Saturday morning.

They showed up at the appointed time, and the redhead looked tense. Her orange freckles stood out on her white face, and she half ran along beside us.

"Is it far?" the dark one asked in her clipped, British way.

"Not too," I said, clipping off the words as she did.

The redhead, it turned out, was a year younger than I, and the dark one, my age.

"How come you're both in the same grade?" I asked her.

"Mummy wrote the school asking that we not be separated."

"But how come she —" I nodded toward the redhead, who was now a few yards ahead of us — " is in our grade?"

The girl looked embarassed. "It seems that the British schools are a year ahead of the Canadian ones. That's why she's moved up."

"That means that you should be —"

" — in the next class, actually."

"Don't you mind?"

"Yes, I do a bit. But I do extra work at home. I've resumed my piano studies, and I paint a little. I'm enrolled in an art class at the Montreal Museum of Fine Arts on Saturdays. My teacher is going to be Arthur Lismer. Have you heard of him?"

"No."

" — And of course I read. And my foster parent here has a typewriter, and has promised to teach me typing."

Whew!

"Keep track of these streets so you'll be able to find the library whenever you want. We've come along Cote St. Antoine to Claremont. Now we're going down Claremont to Sherbrooke St. Then we'll go along Sherbrooke till we get to Westmount Park. The library's a big red brick building right at the entrance to the park."

As we walked, I grew curious about her.

"Were you scared coming over on the ship from England?" I asked.

"Not scared so much as sick. We had a rough crossing. When we weren't vomiting, my sister and I watched the porpoises playing near the ship. They were great fun. And we saw icebergs; and took part in lifeboat drills."

Though I knew I risked stirring painful memories, I asked, "Were you in the war?"

"Do you mean were we bombed?"

"Yes."

"No. But we had to carry gas masks wherever we went, and wear handkerchiefs on our arms, and identification tags, and cover electric torches with tissue paper to get about in the blackout."

"What was it like — the blackout?"

"Not very pleasant," she said briskly, "However, they put rings of white paint around the lampposts, and reduced the speed limit to 20 miles an hour — that was to help prevent traffic accidents. And cars were fitted with blackout shields, to keep the light beams from shining upward. Train windows were painted black or navy blue so that the light could be on inside the coaches. Oh, and they took down all the road signs, which made things quite confusing."

"Sounds like it. Is your father in the service?"

"No, but he and my mother are in the Home Guard."

"What do they do?"

"I don't quite know exactly. When my sister and I left, my parents were helping to prepare London against attack. But from the middle of July, after we'd arrived here, and all through August, and up until the middle of September, when the Jerries were attacking, they were very busy, Mummy wrote. First the Jerries bombed the Channel, then the harbor, then the countryside, and the airfields, and then London."

"Sounds like you left just in time."

"Things seem to be quiet now, though, thank goodness. My foster mother here tries to keep the newspapers from my sister and me. She didn't want us to read about the bombings. My sister gets nervous, and worries about Mummy and Daddy."

"Were you sorry to leave?"

"Yes, but Mummy was anxious for us to go. Prime Minister Churchill said that a million women were needed for the war industries, and she wanted to do whatever she could, to help, and she said it would be easier for her to do her bit if she didn't have to worry about us.

"Before we left, we went to visit our grandparents, mummy's mother and father, near Brighton, and there were concrete pill boxes all along the beach for soldiers guarding the coastline. And when we visited our grandparents at Wimbledon, my father's parents, we saw that they'd dug up Wimbledon Common and left the earth in heaps on it, so enemy aircraft couldn't land there. And all over London there were Guardian Angels."

"Guardian Angels?" I knew she couldn't be referring to the Guardian Angels that Catholics have hovering invisibly somewhere in the vicinity of their right shoulder, watching over them.

"They're barrage balloons, held up by wires above bridges and buildings to keep enemy aircraft from attacking."

My goodness.

"My father's friend, Fred Stackpool, who used to work with him at *The Montreal Star*, just moved back to London a few months before the war started," I told her.

"He chose a rather bad time to go back."

"I know, but he had just retired, and he always said he wanted to go back to England. My father made a speech at his retirement party, and said 'It was 25 years ago that Fred hitched his wagon to The Star.' " I looked at her for her reaction.

"That's clever."

"Fred Stackpool, and his wife, and her sister, Bea, who lived with them, always came to visit us on New Year's Day, and he always brought me English toffees. Were they ever good!"

"Were they in a red plaid box?"

"Yes."

"Were they called Edinburgh Rock?"

"I'm not sure. They may have been."

"Was there a picture of a castle on the box?"

"I can't remember."

"If there was, they're my favorite."

I was reminded of something that had happened in connection with those candies, and told her about it.

"Once, just after New Year's Day, after the Stackpools had been to visit us and had given me my toffees, another friend of my father's, Bill Anderson, an artist from Toronto, came to stay with us while he looked for a job. He slept in the living-room on the couch that pulls out into a bed. I had left my toffees on top of the bookcase of the secretary desk in the living-room so that I wouldn't be tempted to eat them all the time. That way I made them last longer. Well guess what happened? After Bill Anderson left, I went in to get them, and he'd eaten every one!"

"He'd eaten all your toffees!"

"Yes."

"The pig!"

"Was I ever mad!"

"I can imagine."

"My father was mad too. He gave me the money to buy some Mac-Intosh toffee to take their place. It costs a nickle. It's good too. Really hard, though. You have to keep it in your mouth a long time to get it soft enough to chew, but it's delicious."

"I must try it some time."

We continued walking, then I said, "You want to hear something funny?"

"What?"

"Do you know that girl in our class that everyone calls Wooly?"

"Yes."

"She's one of my best friends. Anyway, a couple of years ago we had to write a composition about a faraway place, and she wrote a composition about Ingling."

"Ingling?"

"Yes, When she handed it in, the teacher said, "Ingling? Where's that?" and Wooly said, "Ingling — across the ocean, where the King and Queen live.""

"*Ingling*? She thought it was called Ingling?"

"Yes."

We both laughed — just a little at first, then we stopped walking, crossed our knees, and roared.

I sobered up long enough to say, "I wonder if she's ever heard that song, 'There'll Always Be An Ingling?' And then we laughed some more.

As we turned at Westmount Park, the redhead bounded ahead, "Is this it?" she asked, and took the steps two at a time. She was inside before her sister or I had reached the top of the stairs.

Inside, the redhead was looking all around with a satisfied expression. The tension had left her face, and she looked relaxed for the first time since I'd known her. I guess there was something about the library that made her feel at home. I showed her where the children's section was, and she immediately went off, looking for *Winnie The Pooh*, I guessed.

"I have to get home", I told her sister. "Do you think you can find your way back okay?"

"Oh, yes. We'll just retrace our steps. Thanks awfully. It was smashing of you to bring us here."

I couldn't help smiling. "*Smashing*", I repeated. "That's just like Angela Brazil."

I was still smiling as I walked along Sherbrooke Street toward home. As I was a Girl Guide, I figured that I had done my good deed for the day, and it made me feel ripping, topping, and perfectly spiffing, as Angela Brazil's characters would say.

Montreal Star Aug. 19, 1942

Young British Guests Dance On Arrival

Party of 157 Includes Many From Districts Now Being Raided

From Grimsby and the Thames estuary; from Liverpool, from towns and cities in Britain where the drone of German bombers is now an accustomed noise, 157 children arrived in Montreal today on a boat train from an eastern port.

They danced jigs when they stepped onto the platform of Bonaventure Station, glad to be out and moving after hours on the train. They asked questions about Canada, their war-time homeland, in the accents of half-a-dozen British cities, and again and again did the "thumbs up" gesture that denotes confidence, faith, hope and half-a-dozen other patriotic meanings which English children feel too deeply to talk about.

41 FOR MONTREAL

Of the total that arrived this morning, 41 were bound for Montreal and for distribution to homes in this area. It is understood that 16 of these will go to friends or relatives in the city and that the others will be placed among the volunteer families listed by the Council for Overseas Children. All were moved to the Royal Victoria College, as were a group of 50 others who were bound for points in Western Canada.

The remainder, destined for Ontario points and distribution from Toronto, went on in their special car at 10 a.m.

Three-quarters of these child guests of Canada are being sent out under the British Government scheme, which provides them with free passages. The remaining quarter are also being handled under the Government scheme, but as they come from middle-class families which can afford to pay something, they in most cases paid at least part of the cost of bringing them to Canada.

Courtesy of *The Gazette*, Montreal

CHAPTER FOUR

SUB DEBS AND JUNIOR MISSES

As the school year progressed, Cath and I grew increasingly anxious. Our years in an all girl grammar school had ill prepared us for the time when we would be old enough to date, which, by popular custom would be the following year, when we were in high school.

Though we followed closely the adventures of Henry Aldrich, played by Ezra Stone, on the radio; and of Andy Hardy, played by Mickey Rooney, on film (that is, when we could manage to get in to see the films), we were not persuaded that teenaged boys actually behaved as they did.

"Maybe American teenagers are different from Canadians," Cath suggested.

"Or maybe teenagers in small towns like Carvel (where Andy Hardy lived) are different from teenagers in big cities like Montreal."

"Or maybe it's because we go to an all-girl Catholic school, and they go to a coed public school."

We couldn't account for the differences, but we never saw any teenaged boys driving around in jalopies with messages painted on them like PEACHES, HERE'S YOUR CAN and 7 DAYS IN THIS MAKES ONE

WEAK, as Andy and his pals did; or knew of girls and boys who almost contemplated suicide if they couldn't get a date for the Senior Prom.

We had only gotten as far in our romantic development as the "long-distance crush". That's when you see a boy whose looks you like, and you become fixated on him. You find out his daily routine, then hang around in the background of his life. Usually the boy is hopelessly out of reach — too old, too interested in someone else, too remote.

In my case, it was a boy named Kenny C. who lived on the next street, and was *seventeen* years old. I made friends with a girl who lived up the street from him, and Cath and I would go over and sit on the girl's front steps waiting for him to walk up the street, then we'd discreetly follow him to the A & P, Steinberg's or wherever, as he did errands for his mother.

When we found out he had a job as an usher at the Empress, we would go over to the theatre and stand outside, ostensibly looking at the movie still cards, but hoping for a glimpse of him in uniform. I daydreamed of meeting him, and thought of several ways of bringing it about.

Kenny C. traded his usher's uniform for a Navy uniform without ever having once indicated he was aware that we were both sharing the same planet — and a good thing too, because if he *had* spoken to me, I would have been tongue-tied.

"When you go to an all-girls school you don't get any practice talking with boys," Cath complained. (We knew that the insults we traded with the boys on our street didn't count as conversation.)

"I bet girls who go to public school don't have any trouble talking to boys," I agreed.

Sometimes we went over to the park across from the school and hung around the fringes of groups of boys and girls talking together to see if there were any conversational tricks we might pick up. I noticed an older girl named Gloria, who went to our school, talking to some boys in the park, and she seemed to be getting along fine, so one day I waited for her as she came out of school.

"Gloria," I said, "Can I ask you something?"

"Sure," she said, "What?"

"How do you talk to boys?"

She looked blank for a moment, then said, "The same way you talk to girls."

I didn't believe it. "You do? Really?"

"Sure."

38

"Well what subjects do you talk about then?"

"The same ones you talk about with girls — pretty much."

"I don't know anything about sports. I thought boys always talked about sports."

"You don't have to talk about sports. They can talk about sports with other guys."

"You mean you talk about normal things, the way you do with your friends?"

"Of course. My gosh, what do you think boys are — from another planet or something?"

Well, maybe. I had read the book, *Seventeen*, by Booth Tarkington, and the heroine spoke baby-talk to boys, and all the boys were after her. I wondered if perhaps I would have to say "ess" for yes and "milyums" for millions, and "whatcums" for what, and be arch and coy as she was, in order to be popular too. I thought I might have to take lessons in cute, and start practicing nose-wrinkling — a price I wasn't sure I was willing to pay for popularity.

I had observed too, one popular girl at the park who developed an extra "ha" in her laugh when boys were around. Generally she laughed "ha-ha-ha" like everybody else, but when she was talking to a boy, she'd go, "ha-ha-(hiccup-sound)-ha". I guessed it was supposed to make her sound cuter or something. It sounded phony to me, but it seemed to work with the boys because they flocked around her and seemed to be making every effort to get her to laugh more. So it was a real relief to hear from Gloria that I shouldn't have any trouble talking to boys.

When I reported the conversation back to Cath, she looked skeptical and said tersely, "I hope she's right."

... with dates galore! Smart Sub-Debs know how to make that happy ending come true. Just order the booklets listed below and see how you, too, can become the gal that rates No. 1 with all the fellows.

JOURNAL REFERENCE LIBRARY

YOUR DATE-ABILITY

1658. Do Boys Like You? If not, why not? Find out how you can improve. 5c.
2269. How About a Date? How to hear that sweet phrase often. 5c.
1532. Know Your Man. And how to handle him. Some subtle hints. 5c.
1669. Going Steady. How to hold him. 5c.
1228. Rating for Dating. Are you a drip-date? Find out what to do about it. 5c.

YOUR DOINGS

2270. Nix on Necking. It's not done and why. 5c.
2272. Memo for Manners. Bright behavior at home, on parties, on dates. Make sure you know what to do when. 5c.
1344. Act Your Age! Of course you're growing up, but are you really out of rompers? 5c.
2276. Sub-Deb Club Handbook. Need pointers for your club? Here are the answers. 5c.
2225. Fun and Funds. New ideas to swell your club treasury and put your club in the spotlight. 5c.
2306. Speak Up! Does conversation bother you? Well, learn to speak up. 5c.

YOUR LOOKS

2253. Let's Be Lovely. Grooming tips to give you that clean, well-scrubbed, rosy, fresh look that fellows like. 5c.
1207. Mirror Magic. Your skin, your make-up, your eyes, your smile—how to make them the kind you want to see in your mirror. 5c.
2268. Glamour for Glasses. Complete with sketches to help you choose the right shape and shade for you. 5c.
2277. Facts About Figures. Pounds in the wrong places? Exercises will help you. 5c.
2322. Clothes Check-Up! What you should wear. 5c.
2324. Count Your Calories. And keep those extra pounds off your figure. 5c.

1378. The Way You Wear Your Hair. The style for you. 5c.

YOUR PERSONALITY

1022. How to be Popular. The real low-down. 5c.
2275. Don't Shy Away. Bolster your self-confidence. You may be missing out. 5c.
1539. Do Girls Like You? If not, find out why. 5c.
1514. Personality Report Card. Rate yourself. 5c.

YOUR FUN

1515. Fun Outdoors. Picnics, hikes—open-air fun. 5c.
2254. It's a Date for a Party. One for every holiday of the year. 5c.
1504. Let's Eat. What to serve. 5c.
1377. Games to Play. Pep up your gatherings with some new fun ideas. 10c.
2210. Let's Have a Party. For every occasion. Eight complete plans. 5c.
1691. Halloween Antics. Tricks and stunts for Halloween parties. 5c.
2307. Dance Doin's. A prom coming up? Make this one different. 5c.
1303. Let's Dance. Dance plans de luxe. 5c.
2271. Banquets to Give. Ideas for initiation and Junior-Senior banquets—everything from centerpieces to favors and nut cups. 10c.
2308. Sixteen. A one-act play for six girls and four fellows. Playing time, 30 minutes. 10c.
2309. Objective Johnny. A one-act comedy for three girls and two fellows. 10c.

FOR YOUR MEN

1192. Gentlemen Preferred. A book you can pass on to him—etiquette for the man in your life. 5c.
1668. Know Your Girl. Tips on types and what to do about each. 5c.
1546. If I Were a Man! Some inside information on what a gal expects. 5c.

We will gladly send any of these booklets if you'll order by name and number. They will be mailed anywhere in the United States and Canada upon receipt of stamps, cash, check or money order. Do not send stamped, addressed envelopes or Savings Stamps. Readers in all foreign countries should send International Reply Coupons, purchased at their post office. Please address all requests to the Reference Library, Ladies' Home Journal, Philadelphia 5, Penna.

CHAPTER FIVE

MISS DELACEY IS EXPECTING

One day, Lucy, the girl who sat in front of me, curled her hand around her mouth so the teacher couldn't read her lips, and whispered, "Miss DeLacey is expecting. Pass it on."

What! Of all the ridiculous things I'd ever heard. Miss DeLacey wasn't even married! How could she be expecting? I leaned forward and whispered at the back of Lucy's head, "You're crazy!"

The curled hand again. "I'm not. I can tell by the way she looks."

Well I couldn't argue with that. There were 14 kids in Lucy's family. I guess she'd know what someone who is expecting looked like although ... Miss DeLacey didn't stick out in front.

I passed Lucy's observation on by reporting, "Lucy says Miss De-Lacey is expecting. Pass it on."

A sharp intake of breath behind me. "She is *not*."

"Lucy said."

I could hear rustlings and stirrings behind me as the information was passed from girl to girl.

The situation called for a meeting in the school yard at recess, with Lucy at the center of the group.

"I can tell," she insisted, "because her waist is straight up and down, and her chest sticks out more."

"Maybe she's just putting on weight."

"She *is* putting on weight, and its because she's expecting. Her eyes look funny too, the way my mother's do when she's expecting."

I had noticed that Miss DeLacey's bright smile never quite reached her eyes, but that didn't seem to be what Lucy meant.

"Just watch," Lucy promised, "pretty soon she'll start to wear loose blouses, and her stomach will stick out."

Then one day, sure enough, Miss DeLacey was wearing a boxy top. Lucy gave me a triumphant, I-told-you-so look.

Miss DeLacey had a younger sister named Geraldine who went to the high school that was housed in our elementary school building. Jacquie, a girl in our class, knew one of Geraldine's friends, and one day she came to school with some exciting news.

"Guess what?" she told us in the schoolyard before class, "Miss DeLacey's sister said that Miss DeLacey eloped with a soldier, and now he's overseas!"

— How romantic.

"I wonder why Miss DeLacey doesn't *tell* us she's married. It seems funny calling her Miss DeLacey when she's expecting," I said.

"Maybe," someone speculated, "the teachers here aren't allowed to be married."

She may have had a point. I thought of all the lay teachers who had been in the school, and none of them had been married.

Sometimes while we were all busy writing, and Miss DeLacey didn't have anything to do, I would look at her surreptiously, and see her looking out of the window, with a faraway look. I wondered if at those times she was thinking of her soldier husband.

The kids in the class started being nicer to her. If, for instance, she was about to lift something heavy, Lucy, maybe out of force of habit because of her mother, would run and give her a hand.

Before, when she came into the classroom we were always talking, and it used to take her a while to get us settled down to work, but as her smock tops stuck out further, we started quietening down as soon as she entered the room.

One Monday morning, by the time Miss DeLacey was beginning to sound a bit out of breath when she talked, Jacquie came in and solemnly told us to meet her at recess. She had had word from the friend who knew Miss DeLacey's sister.

"Miss DeLacey's husband was killed overseas," Jacquie reported. We gasped.

"But she came in today!"

"She got the news Friday night," Jacquie said.

"But — but she doesn't look any different!"

"No, she doesn't. You'd think her eyes would be red from crying."

"Maybe she cried all weekend."

"Gee, we can't even tell her we feel sorry, when we're not supposed to know."

"Well we can be nice to her, and not talk in class."

Back in the classroom, I noticed Miss DeLacey's eyes were bright and not red rimmed or swollen. But then they'd always been bright and wide open, as if she were making a conscious effort to keep them that way.

Imagine! There she was — she had gotten married, and kept it a secret; she was expecting and trying to keep that a secret; and now she was a widow, and keeping that a secret too.

When I told my mother the latest sad news, she shook her head and said, "Oh, the poor thing."

Lucy, our expert, said she figured by the way Miss DeLacey looked that the baby would be born sometime that summer.

At least she wouldn't have to take time off from school to have it.

BRITAIN AT WAR
By J. B. PRIESTLEY

What Has the War Done to Us?

London, December 26.—(By Wireless)—What many Americans must now be asking themselves is this: Our people are now at war and what effect will war have on them? It is a very important question. We know that frequently a whole society has rapidly deteriorated during war. Some people would not hesitate to declare that all societies deteriorate during wars.

At any time between 1919 and 1939 I think I would have agreed with those people. I believed myself that all talk of wars regenerating society was militaristic twaddle and that the total influence of war was invariably ruinous. I took that line not merely because I detested war (which I still do) but also because it seemed to me that the effect of the great war on our people had been all to the bad.

Now it is possible that if this present war goes on and the casualty lists soon become like those of the last war, we will find ourselves once more degenerating. This much I am frankly admitting. On the other hand, I am absolutely convinced that up to now the influence of this war on the British people has not only not been bad but has definitely been good.

We are a better people than we were before the war began. I admit I had no high opinion of the state of our society before this war, and I wrote a good deal on the subject. We were becoming less politically minded, a dangerous drift by the folk of a democracy. As a matter of fact, in actual practice we were not a democracy but a plutocracy. And the English public mind was in poor shape. Contrast the queer, hysterical behavior over Munich (a manifestation that puzzled me at the time) with the calm that greeted actual danger when it came.

All the changes that have taken place since the war, in the tone and temper of our society, seem to be good rather than bad. The average Briton is a better citizen. In spite of all the restrictions imposed on his way of living he is, I think, more alive than he was before the war. He is more public-spirited, more thoughtful. It ought to be easier to talk nonsense now to the public and get away with it, but in actual fact it is much harder. People are more, not '--- critical than they were before the war.

The intellectual life of the country, notwithstanding all the wartime difficulties and restrictions, is no worse than it was and the average citizen and his wife tend to take far more interest in world affairs, politics, economics, social reform, reconstruction and the like than they did in peacetime.

Innumerable small study and discussion groups have come into existence during the last two years and much good work is being done in many of them. And the demand for intelligent books now, because of the paper shortage, is far greater than the supply.

Even men in the armed forces, who are worked so hard that they could be forgiven a lack of interest in mental pursuits, are demanding increased educational facilities, more books, more good lectures and more discussions. Some of the most intelligent and searching letters I have had come from men in the forces. The war has not stopped them from thinking. It has made many of them begin to think.

The "eat, drink and be merry, for tomorrow we die" spirit so characteristic of the last war has not been much in evidence in this war. Then London was a kind of maelstrom of pleasure-seeking, but now, although it enjoys itself, it is comparatively sedate. I have seen few signs this year of youngsters flinging aside all restraint. People are now much quieter and more sensible.

And people are kind and considerate. I am always noticing this on the frequent railway journeys I make, which because of the various wartime restrictions usually are very irksome. People are tired, but somehow they do not lose temper and they are wonderfully decent and civilized to each other. The war has increased, not decreased, their mutual consideration.

Though the enemy is far more cruel and vicious than he was in the last war, and has tried to blast hell out of us, our people show no trace of a hysterical, revengeful spirit. (They have even been charged with showing too little of it—and what a compliment that is!) They do not howl and scream for vengeance. They do not lose their heads over either defeat or victory. The mere intoxication of war seems to have passed them by. They are now, on the whole, a sober, thoughtful people, a trifle grim beneath the easy humor.

In all this, then, there is no trace whatever of that deterioration associated with wars. Where there have been changes they are improvements. I would much rather live with these people than the people of Britain in 1938. Nor do I believe that the American people are going to behave very differently in spite of the more electric atmosphere across the Atlantic.
Copyright, 1941, Overseas News Agency.

CHAPTER SIX

HIGHER LEARNING

On my first day of high school, I stood in the auditorium, waiting for the bell to ring, not knowing a single soul. It was my own fault. I could have gone to high school in the same building that housed the elementary school I just graduated from. Its high school was located on the top floor of the building. Indeed, when I had been in the early grades of elementary school, I had thought the term "high school" derived from its lofty location.

I just couldn't face the idea, however, of doing any more time there. A change of venue was clearly indicated, so I enrolled in a downtown high school.

I was leaning against a wall, trying to look nonchalant instead of self-conscious, when I happened to see a nun I had had as a teacher in grade school. I had heard about her being transferred to this school, but hadn't expected to see her quite so soon. I immediately turned to the girl standing next to me and said something, trying to look as if I were engaged in animated conversation, so that the nun wouldn't think I was a social outcast.

I had always had the fear that my teachers would think that no one sought out my company. I dreaded field trips that involved the whole

45

class walking somewhere in ranks. I was always afraid that no one would want to walk beside me, and that I would have to end up walking with the nun.

The girl I picked to talk to in the auditorium turned out to be in my home room. Her name was Pauline, and she was a cynic.

We filed in and took our assigned seats in our home room. Pauline was given the desk across the aisle from me. Our home room teacher, who was, as it turned out, our Religion and English teacher as well, opened up a book of poetry and said, "There's a special reason why Catholics are receptive to poetry. Does anyone know why?"

An idea half formed itself in my mind about how many Catholics were Irish, and so many Irish people had a lyrical way with words, and I tentatively raised my hand. I wasn't as fast as Pauline, though. Her hand shot up immediately.

"Yes?"

"Because so many of our prayers are like poems?"

The teacher nodded and smiled approvingly, and Pauline's face settled into the expression a Catholic student wears when she has not only given the teacher the desired answer; but she managed to sound pious while doing so. She caught me looking at her, and, once the teacher's eyes were off her, gave me a little smirk and whispered from behind her hand, "Tell them what they want to hear."

This philosophy worked well for her I was to discover to my rue, when a few weeks later, our English teacher announced an essay contest sponsored by the Congregation of Notre Dame.

After telling us the contest rules, because I was a reporter on our school newspaper, *The Student Prints*, the teacher turned my way and said, "That sounds right up your alley, Mary."

I *hated* it when a teacher said something like that to me. It had happened before when we were studying Edgar Allan Poe's story, "The Gold Bug". The teacher, before assigning our homework, said at that time "This will appeal to *you* Mary." Then she told us we had to decipher the code used in the story. I worked for *hours* trying to decipher that damn code, and was finally reduced to the ignominy of having to copy it out the next morning before class, from the homework of the quite dull girl who sat in front of me. (If the truth be known, I was never that good at deciphering Radio Orphan Annie's messages on my ROA secret decoder pin, either).

We were to write an essay on a Quebec heroine, and were given a choice of three: Marguerite Bourgeoys, founder of the Congregation of

46

Notre Dame; Madeleine de Verchères, the 14 year old girl who saved her parents' fort from the Iroquois; or Kateri Tekakawitha, an Indian girl known as the "Lily of the Mohawks".

I decided to go with Marguerite Bourgeoys as the subject of my essay, not only because she was dear to the starched bosoms of the contest's sponsors, but also because she was one of the most remarkable women of her time.

I thought I had turned in quite a creditable essay, and felt confident that I stood a good chance of winning in my age category. But when the winning names were announced, mine was not among them. Pauline's, however, was. When I heard her name called, a rush of mouth-drying jealousy suffused me, and when I turned around in surprise to look at her — she was sitting directly behind me — she was wearing the same smug smirk she'd had on her face on the first day of school.

After acknowledging the applause, congratulations, and her prize on the stage of the assembly hall, she returned to her seat, leaned forward, and whispered to the back of my head, "It's all in the last paragraph."

She had also chosen to write about Margeurite Bourgeoys, and she knew that I had too. As the Mother Directress read her essay to the assembled classes, with the taste of ashes in my mouth, I listened carefully for the message in the last paragraph.

I took note that Pauline didn't seem to have any more facts than I had. And the writing wasn't noticeably better than mine. But she had thought of something that I hadn't. Despite my feelings of envy, I had to catch my breath in admiration.

Her last paragraph was a stirring plea for Margeurite's canonization. The Congregation of Notre Dame had been praying for *years* for Marguerite Bourgeoys to be proclaimed a saint. Indeed, it had always been the "special intention" that they had included in our prayers whenever they could. Naturally they were affected favorably by Pauline's emotional endorsement of their cause. She had told them what they wanted to hear.

When we returned to our classroom, Pauline prominently displayed her prize on the top of her desk — the show-off.

*

There were boys in the high school, but if you were caught speaking to one in school, you were suspended. I could never see how such a crime could be committed anyway, because the boys' section and girls' section were hermetically sealed off from one another like two separate schools, the girl's side being run by the nuns, and the boys' side by the Christian Brothers.

The only time I ever saw the boys was when the school put on a Gilbert and Sullivan operetta, and there were boys and girls in the cast. They must have been given special dispensation from St. Genesius, the patron saint of performers.

Even as a reporter for the school paper I turned in my copy to a teacher, and never got so much as a peek at the boy editor.

We had only a half hour for lunch, and there was no leaving the premises. That way the boys and girls couldn't even catch a glimpse of each other, let alone meet.

Another precaution taken by the Mother Directress and Brother Director so that the boys and girls didn't come in contact with one another, was that the girls were let out of school earlier than the boys. The nuns knew that the young ladies would never hang around outside the school waiting for the boys, and the nuns were right. The girls didn't hang around outside the school waiting for the boys; they went down to the soda fountain at the corner of Park and Pine, and waited for them there.

I always went straight home myself, not out of any great desire to adhere to the school's rules, but in order to hear a radio program that came out of Chicago called "Club Matinee".

It was hosted by a man with a nasal voice named Ransom Sherman, whom we affectionately referred to as Rancid Sherman. The announcer was Durward Kirby, whose picture Cath had sent away for the year before, and had hanging on her bedroom door.

Ransom Sherman said things that killed us, like "Ransom Sherman's latest picture can be seen on his mother's dresser." And his conversation was sprinkled with non-sequiturs like: "Send in your coupon — today!" "Don't let this happen — to you!" "Let us not say things we will regret later." "My advice to you is to *go* to these people and ask their forgiveness." and, "*Tell* me about yourself, your hopes, your dreams, your ambitions."

Cath and I listened to the program in our respective homes, and when it was over, got together and went about our after-school activities, repeating these Shermanisms all the while.

This is a strange Christmas Eve. Almost the whole world is locked in deadly struggle, and, with the most terrible weapons which science can devise, the nations advance upon each other. Amid all the tumult, we have tonight the peace of the spirit in each cottage home and in every generous heart. Therefore we may cast aside for this night at least the cares and dangers which beset us, and make for the children an evening of happiness in a world of storm. And so, in God's mercy, a happy Christmas to you all.

Winston Churchill
Washington, D.C.
Dec. 24, 1941

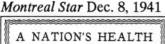

```
A NATION'S HEALTH
      ·IS
A NATION'S WEALTH
```

JAPAN FORCES WORLD WAR

WITH a dastardly treachery that is quite in keeping with her modern diplomacy, Japan struck suddenly with the venom of a poisonous snake at American and British bases in the Pacific yesterday, at the very moment when her peace envoys were professedly seeking to continue negotiations with President Roosevelt. Thus the flames of war are spread around the world, and the menace of its horrors draws closer and closer to Canada's back door.

We must await clarification before we can properly assess Japanese strategy, but at the time of writing it seems quite clear that the Japanese have pursued the same ingeniously deceptive methods they originated in Manchuria. It was Japan who, in that ill-fated land, lit the match that has since set the world on fire. Her technique gave Hitler and Mussolini the lead which both subsequently followed. Infiltrations of troops made over a long period with the avowed object of protection, accompanied with repeated protestations of determination to maintain peace in the Orient, hoodwinked the diplomats of Western Powers. There was one exception, Mr. H. L. Stimson, U.S. Secretary of State for War, who saw through the wily Orientals' far-sighted plan and who invited Britain to join the United States in foiling Tokio. At that time, however, Britain did not see her way owing to preoccupations elsewhere to act.

Mussolini took a page out of Japan's book. He followed her example of ruthlessness and cold-blooded murder in Abyssinia, and Hitler, who had all the time been watching and studying, in his turn did the same in Europe. Now the Japanese, doubtless recalling their success in Manchuria, have repeated the plan with swift and startling suddenness, and it cannot be denied with material initial gain. They struck over a vast area of the Pacific seemingly from bases in French Indo-China and Japan, and from various islands which, by a strange irony of fate, were mandated to Japan under the Treaty of Versailles. They struck as far to the east as Hawaii, five thousand miles from Indo-China, and submarines are reported within one thousand miles of the

Shopping Days
to
CHRISTMAS

More Bedtime Stories

London Bombings Act as Spur for Children's Tales

MOUNTAIN VIEW, Cal., Dec. 19 ·—(U.P.)— Nightly bombardment of London apparently has increased the demand for bedtime stories for children. While the bombing was at its height, Arthur S. Maxwell, author of "Uncle Arthur's Bedtime Stories" received the following cable from his London publishers:

"Imperative receive manuscript bedtime stories before October."

Maxwell cabled in reply: "Courage, copy coming."

CHAPTER SEVEN

PUBLIC SERVICE ADS

"Listen to this," my mother said gleefully, as she was leafing through Collier's magazine at the kitchen table. "It's one of those public service ads."

After the United States had entered the war on December 8th, 1941, that type of ad was cropping up in all the magazines. They were paid for by corporations that had been converted to the making of essential materials for the war effort. The messages were published, supposedly to speed American victory, but as an added bonus, they helped keep the corporation's name before the public. This one had been paid for by the Stewart-Warner Corporation.

It says, "WANT TO BUILD A BOMBER RIGHT IN YOUR OWN KITCHEN? If you think there isn't anything else you can do to help win the war, walk into your own kitchen. There isn't a kitchen like that anywhere else in this world. A gleaming white refrigerator that actually makes ice and keeps your food fresh — at a snap of a switch. A beautiful compact range to make cooking easier...Over there, a spotless white sink and perhaps a dishwasher. Your toaster — waffle iron — food mixer — vacuum cleaner. Nowhere else in the world do women have such luxuries".

We both looked around. I put my hand on my hip and sashayed around, languidly indicating with the other hand all of the wonders that supposedly graced this gorgeous kitchen.

Our "gleaming white refrigerator that actually made ice" was an ice box with a block of ice in it that actually melted into the drip pan underneath.

Our green and cream McClary's range hardly fit the "beautiful and compact" description. My mother's dishwasher was at that moment sashaying around the room with her hand on her hip. Our toaster was the kind with two sides that you pulled down in order to get the burnt toast out, beside which we kept a tube of Ozonal to apply to our burnt fingers. We didn't have any waffle iron. Our food mixer was sitting at the table reading Collier's. We did have a vacuum cleaner — the Eureka we'd brought with us from Mimico when we moved to Montreal when I was four.

My mother read on, "Or glance out the window at your car. Streamline — powerful — ready to carry you in comfort wherever you want to go."

I went over to the kitchen window and peered around for sight of the streamlined car, shielding my eyes against the glare of its gleaming chrome. There was none. Streamlined or otherwise.

My mother then read the pledge that she, as a housewife, was urged in the ad to make. All of the things suggested, such as, "adjusting food, clothing, and fuel purchases to the level of necessity," and "accepting sacrifice and privation without complaint," she'd been doing through the Depression years anyway, and now she was doing it again through the war. "So nu?" — as Mrs. Nussbaum in Allen's Alley would say, "What then?"

"This (the ad) reminds me of a joke I heard once," my mother said, "about a rich young man who gets to be a radio producer, and his boss tells him he's to produce a show that will be on every Sunday afternoon at five o'clock, and the producer says, "What? — when everyone's playing polo?"

Wear this uniform proudly,
Mrs. _____

 . . . It's just a kitchen apron. Not a bit dramatic. Yet you who wear it perform a service without which this war cannot be won. Mending, painting, making things do. Planning good meals with rationed foods. Keeping everyone on the job. Holding home together, no matter what. Yes . . . it's just a kitchen apron . . . but it's your badge of service. Wear it proudly.

Save this newspaper!

WHO would have thought you'd be a deserter from a dustmop . . . when Mom's counting on you? When you *country's* counting on you? . .

As Mom explained—it's girls like you taking on "homework" who release *a whole army of mothers* for rolling bandages and selling war bonds and driving drill presses.

That's how important you are . . . but look at you now!

CANADA NEEDS YOU STRONG

EAT THESE FOODS DAILY—PLUS OTHERS!

FRUITS—One serving of tomatoes daily, or of a citrus fruit, or of tomato or citrus fruit juices, and one serving of other fruits, fresh, canned, or dried.

VEGETABLES — (In addition to potatoes, of which you need one serving daily) —Two servings daily of vegetables, preferably leafy green, or yellow, and frequently raw.

MILK — Adults: one-half pint. Children: more than one pint. And some cheese.

CEREALS and BREAD—One serving of a whole grain cereal and four to six slices of Canada-approved bread, brown or white.

MEAT, FISH, EGGS, etc.—One serving a day of meat, fish, or meat substitutes. Liver, heart, or kidney once a week. Eggs, at least three or four weekly.

Canadian Nutrition Programme

CHAPTER EIGHT

GOOD CATHOLIC BOYS

Cath and I palled around with two other girls named Mitt and Wooly. We had all gone through elementary school together, but while Cath and I had gone on to different high schools, they had remained at the school in N.D.G.

It was Mitt who heard about the Friday night dances in the gym of the Catholic boy's school in N.D.G.

"Girls go with their girl friends, and boys go with their boy friends, and then you dance together when you get there," she told us.

The first such dance we went to was on the evening of my brother Choate's wedding. He was in the Army, and only had a seven day leave for the honeymoon — he and his new bride left the reception as soon as they politely could. I was glad, being all dressed up, to have some place to go.

As we four girls stood together uncertainly, I noticed a boy looking in my direction. A former Mary Todd might have snippily said at his stare, "I hope you *know* me the next time," but the new, demure Mary Todd returned his look briefly, then glanced away. He came over.

"Want to jive?" he asked.

I took his extended hand. The dance we did was the Lindy. Cath, Mitt, Wooly, and I had been practicing it together for weeks.

Because the dance was being held in a Catholic school, all of the boys we met were Catholic. "Good Catholic boys", was how our mothers described them. From your mother, a boy automatically earned the modifier "good" merely by being Catholic, just as from a journalist a Catholic automatically earned the modifier "devout".

And, as Mark Twain had once heard of a church choir that was *not* ill bred, "but it was a great many years ago and in some foreign country", so, too, would our mothers concede that perhaps there was a Catholic boy who was *not* "good", but that, too, would have been in another time and another place.

At that very first dance, Cath, Mitt, Wooly, and I were launched socially. We had become, as *The Ladies' Home Journal* had it, Sub Debs. Boys had entered our lives. And particularly in Cath's case, they had better be Catholic.

Cath's mother developed an uncanny ability for determining whether or not a boy Cath dated was Catholic. I could never understand how she did it. Perhaps she frisked them at the door for scapular medals.

She had a name for boys who didn't pass the test — non-Catholics. (This term included Protestants, Jews, Hindus, Buddhists, Confucianists, Shintoists, and Moslems).

But she wasn't even content if a boy checked out Catholic. She preferred them to be Irish Catholic. Not that she was satisfied if his family came from Ireland. She was concerned as to which *part* of Ireland. Thus, she would have a conversation like this with a boy who bore a recognizably Irish name:

She would repeat the name, rolling it around on her tongue, "Bourke. Now is that Northern or Southern Ireland?" If it was the boy's misfortune to have to say, "Northern", the look on her face would prompt a hasty explanation from him.

Sometimes if a boy said, "Southern", he still wasn't off the hook. "What county?" she wanted to know. If she was familiar with the county, so much the better. If she knew families there, better still. But I used to think as I observed these inquisitions, that Cath should get the boy out of the flat before her mother took it far enough to establish them as relatives, in which case their date would take on a different dimension.

Throughout these third degree sessions, Cath always reacted to her mother's grilling with an exasperated, impatient intake of breath which seemed to be the oral equivalent of stamping her foot.

But one evening Cath's mother hit the jackpot. Cath's date was a polite boy who made the mistake of saying he thought he remembered his mother's mentioning the county where Cath's mother's ancestral home was located.

"And did she happen to mention the O'Days by any chance?"

"I — I can't remember."

"The Neals? The O'Neals? The McNeals?" — She seemed to be conjugating the name Neal.

"I'm not sure."

"What about the Cuddihys? The Shaughnessys? The Houllihys?"

"They sound fam —"

" — The Sullivans? The Monahans? Or the Houllihans?"

"Gosh, I —"

"The Cahills. The Meenaghs? The Tennessys?"

Finally, in a fit of compassion, Cath grabbed the hapless lad by the arm and propelled him out the front door. But I thought I heard, as we walked up the street, Cath's mother's voice trailing after us wistfully, "The Doyles? The Boyles? The Foyles?"...

DIEPPE

Successful Conclusion Of Operation Announced

Canadians Spearhead Tremendous Raid

Main Objectives in Attack
Said to Have Been Achieved

LONDON, Aug. 19—(B.U.P.)—British, Canadian and American commandos carried out a nine-hour raid today on the Dieppe coast of France and withdrew "as planned," it was announced officially tonight.

A total of 95 Allied planes were reported missing and 21 fighter pilots were reported to have made safe landings.

"Some tanks have been lost during the action ashore," the communique said. "Reports show the fighting to have been very fierce. Casualties are likely to be heavy.

The communique reported that 72 German planes were known to be destroyed in addition to several shot down by naval vessels. More than 100 German planes were recorded as "probably destroyed or damaged."

LONDON, Aug. 19—Canadian and Allied Commandos were believed late today still fighting against Nazis in fortified positions about Dieppe as night drew nigh on the French coast, and it was made known that the chief objectives of the great raid had been achieved.

The Canadians, forming one-third of this force, were said to have fought with their traditional courage and initiative in their first brush with the Nazis.

For the first time the Commandos used tanks to smash German gun fortifications and destroy ammunition dumps.

CHAPTER NINE

EAST OF MORGAN'S

At the end of the school year when the results of our final exams came out, I was given mixed reviews. I had done well in English literature, composition, and Latin, but poorly in math and algebra. So poorly, in fact, that enclosed with my report card was a notice that I would have to take a supplementary exam in algebra at summer's end, to determine whether or not I would pass to the next grade.

The boy named Jack that I "went around with" that summer, did his best to tutor me for the exam. It was unfortunate for me that my brother Choate, the mathematical wizard of our family, was away in the Army. He could just look at a column of figures and tell you the correct total in seconds. He had been studying for his C.A. when he joined up.

He might have been able to provide some key to what, to me, was the mystery of algebra. But Jack did the best he could, considering what he had to work with, which was a girl whose brain turned to blanc mange as soon as she saw numbers. He came over almost every day between caddying jobs, to sit on the front steps and help me.

It didn't do much good though. When I took the supplementary exam, I stared at most of the questions blankly.

After the exam, another girl, who had also taken a supp, and I, walked out of the building together. We discussed our respective exams, and apparently she hadn't done any better at hers than I had at mine. I knew her only slightly. Her name was Libby. She was a couple of years older than I, and I had seen her a few times in the assembly hall.

As we came out onto the school steps, she said, "Feel like going to a movie?"

"I only have a bus ticket to get home."

"That's okay," she said, "I've got tons of dough." And did she ever: she opened her purse to give me a glimpse, and my eyes popped as I saw the bills inside.

We walked down to Park and Pine, and she bought a paper to see what was on. There was a triple bill that looked good, but it was in a crummy theatre on Ste. Catherine Street East.

"Why not go there?" she suggested.

"It's supposed to be a really crappy place," I said.

"It's not so bad," she said, "I go there a lot."

"My mother would throw a seven if she ever found out I went."

"So how's she going to find out?"

"Besides, I don't have a Registration card."

"Oh, that doesn't matter. They *never* ask for your card there."

I wavered. One of the pictures playing was "Bahama Passage" with Sterling Hayden and Madeleine Carroll. Sterling Hayden was the big heartthrob of the moment, so I caved in.

She put a streetcar ticket in for me and the car travelled down Park Avenue to St. Catherine Street. Once on Ste. Catherine, we started walking east to Ste. Lawrence Boulevard, known as "The Main", the street that bisected Montreal into East and West. We were now proceeding east of The Main, unfamiliar territory for me. There were pool halls, pinball machine arcades, taverns, tatoo parlors, and places that sold hot dogs.

"Want a steamie?" Libby asked.

"A what?"

"A steamed hot dog. I'll pay."

"Oh. Okay." We stopped, and she ordered for the two of us. It was different from the hot dogs I was used to. Piled on it were mustard, pickles, onions, shredded lettuce, tomatoes, and I don't know what else. It took a while to eat, and when we had finished, we had reached the theatre.

It didn't look like much from the outside, and inside, it was worse. There were a few patrons scattered here and there, some of whom looked as if they had come in to sleep. We took our seats as far away as possible from these bums and rubbydubs. I made sure I sat in an aisle seat.

"Bahama Passage" was just starting, and Libby got up and walked back to the lobby for some candy. I was nervous, sitting alone till she got back.

Within a matter of moments after her return to the seat, a middle-aged man, smelling like a brewery, made his way along the line of empty seats in our row, and sat down beside Libby. If a director had phoned Central Casting for a seedy looking type, they would have sent him. He epitomized the "strangers" my mother had always warned me not to talk to.

I immediately crossed my legs and hunched my shoulders, and swivelled as far away from them as possible, sneaking a quick look at Libby to see what we should do. With every seat in the row empty, there was no reason for him to ignore them and sit down beside her. What I saw out of the corner of my eye absolutely floored me. She was smiling at him encouragingly, and could it be *flirtatiously*? A creepy looking guy old enough to be her *father*? Then I thought she might know him, but his opening line was, "And why are two such pretty girls sitting all by themselves?" and my heart sank.

Libby tossed her head coquettishly. My God, she looked like Scarlett O'Hara flirting with the Tarleton twins. In a minute she'd be saying, "Fiddledeedee." I was beginning to feel nervous and nauseated, so I jumped up and mumbled to Libby, "I'm going to the bathroom," then raced up the aisle.

The ladies room was so filthy, if you had to flush the john, you'd flush it with your foot. But I wouldn't have used it if you'd paid me. I just stood in front of the mottled mirror, holding my head, and trying to think.

My brain hadn't been functioning during the algebra test, and my judgement had been off in agreeing to come here. Now it was time to do something smart for a change. The queasy feeling in my stomach wasn't just due to the sleazy man; it was guilt for coming to such an unsavory place. It was quite true that my mother would have had a fit, had she known I was there. What to do? I decided to go and whisper to Libby that I thought we should leave, not just change seats. Who could enjoy a movie with all those creeps around anyway?

The decision made, I walked back down the aisle. The man, by this time, had a hand lying idly on the back of her chair. I was afraid to check where the other hand might be.

I leaned into the aisle past my empty seat and whispered to Libby, "I think we'd better go."

She looked surprised. "Go? Why? The movie's just started."

"Well, I —" I looked at her and indicated the man with my chin. She either didn't understand, or pretended not to.

"Well, I'm going," I said, and bolted up the aisle, out of the theatre, and onto Ste. Cathrine Street, where I started running, weaving in and out among the pedestrians until I reached the haven of Morgan's Department Store. Ah, Morgan's. Nice, safe Morgan's. The world east of it was a scary place for me. Too mysterious, exotic, and rich for my blood. I didn't feel at home, welcome or safe there.

As I walked up to Sherbrooke Street to take the bus, I thought, uneasily, of Libby. How dumb could you get? It would have been bad news for her to have allowed a boy her own age to pick her up in such a place, and get so "familiar" with her, as my mother would say. But to be picked up by a *man* — that was bad news with jam on it.

Within a few days I received word that I had failed my algebra exam. I never heard how Libby did.

White Paper Denies Immorality Among British Women's Services

By TANIA LONG.

(Special Cable to The New York Times and The Gazette.)

London, September 2.—Charges that immorality and drunkenness were widespread in three British women's services, which have been voiced from time to time since the units were first organized, are officially denied in a white paper to be made public tomorrow. The report is the result of a four-month investigation conducted by a government-appointed committee consisting of five women and three men under the chairmanship of Violet Markham.

Vague rumors and shadowy gossip to the effect that girls and women in the Auxiliary Territorial Service, the Women's Auxiliary Air Force and the Women's Royal Naval Service were conducting themselves discreditably had agitated public opinion for nearly three years when the government decided to institute an inquiry into the truth or falsehood of the allegations. The investigation included visits to 123 camps and a study of innumerable letters from members of the women's services to their families.

Reporting that it can find no justification for sweeping charges of immorality among the girls, the committee says that such allegations generally resolve themselves "into one or two cases which in the course of gossip have been multiplied times over. The committee reports that the same applies to charges of drunkenness.

"The woman in uniform becomes an easy target for careless talk,' the report says. "To be seen drinking a glass of beer in a public house is to provide the text for fluent remarks about the low standards of the services."

The committee also puts an end once and for all to the story that the illegitimate birthrate in the women's services is far higher than among the civilian population. On the contrary, it is lower, the report says, and gives comparative figures for illegitimate births among the A.T.S. and among civilians of the age groups from which the girls of the A.T.S. are recruited. The pregnancy rate among single A.T.S. girls is 15.4 per 1,000, whereas the rate among the civilian girls is 21.8 per cent. per 1,000 per annum.

Admitting that pregnancy figures may not in themselves be conclusive regarding standards of morality, the committee goes on to point out that a knowledge of birth control has become widespread in recent years and that standards of sexual behavior have greatly changed since Victorian days.

On the whole the committee has found that relations between men and women have been put on a healthy normal basis through their having to work together in the services.

"Service conditions . . . are corrective rather than incitement to bad conduct," the report continues. "There may at times be emotional stresses due to the war which lead to extramarital relationships, but no view would be more false than to imagine that they are typical of the services as a whole."

The charges of drunkenness are equally untrue, the report says. While liquor flows in a volume unknown in the past these days, it is not necessarily drunk to excess, and as for the girls "alcohol has become a symbol of conviviality for women no less than for men," it adds.

Summing up, the committee says that the allegations "reflect most unfairly as a generalization of a body of women in the vast majority of whom are serving their country in a high self-respecting spirit."

"The committee can only deplore the irresponsible conduct of persons who without any first-hand knowledge are content to damage the war effort by malicious and careless talk." it concludes.

Are you in the know?

What to do if Mom says you're too young for dating?

☐ *Try crowd psychology* ☐ *Play Hannah the Hermit* ☐ *Stick to hen parties*

Chances are, it's *solo* dates the family vetoes ... they're not against your having friends. Why not get your schoolmates to rally at your homestead, now and then? Show Mom you can cope with a mixed crowd. Dating first on the "gang" plan is good practice for solos later.

What's the latest "dorm" doings?

☐ *Snack smuggling*
☐ *Platter spinning*
☐ *Briefing-sessions*

Even "dorm" life can be beautiful! Main idea's to be comfortable, though, say campus queens.

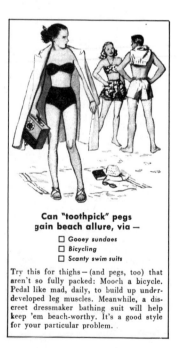

Can "toothpick" pegs gain beach allure, via —

☐ *Gooey sundaes*
☐ *Bicycling*
☐ *Scanty swim suits*

Try this for thighs—(and pegs, too) that aren't so fully packed: Mooch a bicycle. Pedal like mad, daily, to build up under-developed leg muscles. Meanwhile, a discreet dressmaker bathing suit will help keep 'em beach-worthy. It's a good style for your particular problem. .

CHAPTER TEN

DECISION

When the results of my algebra supp came in, my mother, father, and I sat down at the dining-room table after dinner to decide my fate. We had never done anything like that before, nor, as it turned out, would we again, but with my future at stake, serious dicussion was called for.

The facts were laid out on the dining-room table. I had not even come close to passing my algebra exam, so there was no possibility of the school "putting me up" to the next year. If I was to stay in the classical course, I would have to repeat the entire academic year. When I had, would I be assured of passing algebra? There were no guarantees. And should I pass it, what would I do when I encountered geometry and trigonometry?

My parents must have wondered how they could have produced a mathematical wizard in my brother Choate, and a mathematical moron in me.

Another option was for me to switch from the classical course, which featured algebra and Latin, to the commercial high school course which concentrated on shorthand and typing. That way I would be spared having to take algebra, but would be deprived of taking Latin, a subject I enjoyed. Though I had never done well in French, I had discovered I had an aptitude for Latin. I liked the challenge of tracking down the origins of English words from their Latin ancestors; and of figuring out the meaning of English words we hadn't seen before, from their Latin clues. It made me feel like Mr. Keen — Tracer of Lost Parsings.

Further, if I took the commercial high school course, it would rule out my going to college, where I had planned to take journalism, to prepare myself to become first a newspaper reporter, and, ultimately, a foreign correspondent.

"I know a lot of reporters at The Star who never went to journalism school," my father assured me. Then after a pause, "You could take journalism courses at night, did you know that?" I didn't know that.

"The commercial course seems more practical for what you want to do," my mother said.

"But I wouldn't get Latin," I pointed out.

"Shorthand and typing would come in a lot handier for a foreign correspondent than Latin would," she said.

"Unless there was some sort of ruckus at the Vatican," my father put in, and my mother gave him a look.

"Anyway," my practical mother went on, "it would be some time before you would be able to be a foreign correspondent. In the meantime, if you can type and take shorthand, you can always get a job as a stenographer or secretary."

Sitting there at the dining-room table, I felt the mystique of college life that Cath and I talked about, slipping away. Our highest accolade was to describe something as being "collegiate". We knew all about what college life was like. We had gleaned our information from college movies and the college issue of Mademoiselle magazine that came out every fall.

We knew about the tea dances; the importance of getting into the right sorority, the necessity of having a date for the prom, and if it was a Big Man On Campus, so much the better; and the value of a rousing pep rally to inspire the team, because the most important thing of all was for the college football team to win the Big Game against its arch rival.

"If I take the commercial course," I said, "I'm not going back to high school to take it. I'll go to a business college instead."

I enrolled at Sir George Williams Business College, which shared the same building on Drummond St. above Ste. Catherine, as Sir George Williams College. Even though it was a cement campus, with no dry leaves to scuff through, I would at least get a small sense of college life by reading the college newspaper, *The Georgian*; using the college library; and going to some of the college dances.

In addition to the commercial subjects, like shorthand, typing, filing and learning how to operate office equipment, such as dictaphones and adding machines, I also took English literature, composition, spelling, grammar, and "simple arithmetic", for me a contradictory term.

And mirabile dictu, there were boys in my class!

I was thrilled too, that we didn't have to wear a uniform, but the teachers kept emphasizing the importance of preparing for life in the business world, and to that end, we were supposed to wear the same kind of clothes to school that we'd eventually be wearing to work.

Instead, I wore what every other girl my age wore. It was a costume worn by the girls in college as well: a Sloppy Joe sweater, (bought several sizes too large, and worn with the sleeves pushed up); a skirt, generally plaid, or matching the sweater, often pleated, coming to mid-knee or slightly above; pearls, or a detachable white Peter Pan collar; white socks, and brown and white scuffed saddle shoes, or polished loafers.

There was even a verse then current among the teenage set, about the sweaters, that Cath and I were wont to recite:

Ashes to ashes
Dust to dust
If you don't like my Sloppy Joe sweater
Take your hand off my fraternity pin.

And though Cath went to high school and I to business college, there was very little difference in how we spent the rest of the school day. We rode on the same streetcar together to and from school, she getting off at a girl's high school in Westmount, and I continuing on to Drummond Street. Then as soon as she got home she changed into her skirt and Sloppy Joe sweater, and we did all our after school things together.

One of those after school activities was to go to the LaSalle record store near the corner of our street, choose a stack of 78 RPM records from the racks, take them into a listening booth, and play them over and over, until we approached the point of asphyxiation. When we were all listened out, we handed all the records to the cute curly-haired boy who worked there, and said:

"Sorry, we couldn't find anything we wanted."

Or, "We'll buy one when we get our allowance."

Lies. Neither of us owned a phonograph.

We listened to records of the bands of Harry James, Duke Ellington, Woody Herman, Charlie Barnet, and Artie Shaw, but our favorite was Glenn Miller's. It was first given a wide audience in the Spring of 1939, when it did remote radio broadcasts from Frank Dailey's Meadowbrook in New Jersey, "just off the Pompton Turnpike"; and that summer from the Glen Island Casino in New Rochelle, N.Y., where they did ten broadcasts a week. We first heard his records in the summer of 1939 at the YMCA grounds on Hampton Avenue in N.D.G. Every Tuesday and Thursday evening, under the blanket name of "The Bonfire", the city of Montreal put on shows featuring vaudeville acts and silent movies, which were attended by four thousand kids.

There was no bonfire, but after the little kids had gone home, there was a dance for the teenagers. We had been too young to go to the dance, but we stood around the fringes, watching the dancers Shag, Lindy, and Jitterbug to Glenn Miller records like "Sunrise Serenade", "Moonlight Serenade", "Little Brown Jug", and "In The Mood". His distinctive scoring for reeds was a brand new musical sound that people of every age appreciated.

For those of us who had grown up listening to comedy programs on the radio that featured bands that played every song at the same fast-paced tempo, in order to keep the show lively, it was a refreshing change to hear the sweet, saxy, gently swinging sound of Glenn Miller's orchestra.

In the winter of 1939, he began his run on the Chesterfield Show, three nights a week. Cath and I listened to it faithfully till the end of September, 1942, when he did his last broadcast, before going into the Army Air Force. As soon as that last broadcast was over, Cath phoned me, and the two of us cried on the phone together.

We switched our focus from bands to singer at the beginning of 1942, when we picked up a copy of "Night And Day" on the Bluebird label, which sold for 50¢, as opposed to the 75¢ that Victor records cost. We took it into the booth to play, and came reeling out much later, groggy, not only from the lack of air in the booth, but from being "sent".

As Axel Stordahl's lush strings started up, we were unprepared for the onslaught to our senses that the singer's opening phrases would have.

"Jeepers, creepers," Cath breathed.

"Oh my God," I prayed, "I'm getting it."

"But you have nothing to play it on," Cath pointed out.

"I don't care," I said, "I just want to have it."

The boy in the record store was startled. "Your folks finally came through with your allowance, eh?" he said.

From that moment on, we were bonded to Frank Sinatra, who would be the male singer to whom we would compare all others, and always find them wanting.

TROPHIES: Beurling's Got Plenty

From Malta comes this glimpse of Pilot Officer George E. (Lucky) Beurling, of Verdun, Canada's most-decorated fighter pilot of the war and hero of embattled Malta, a belt of cartridges over his shoulder and trophies on either side. Nothing of his whereabouts has been mentioned in news cables since Friday night, strengthening reports he may be coming home shortly from Britain.

Courtesy of *The Gazette*, Montreal

CHAPTER ELEVEN

TOUTE LA GANG AT THE MOVIES

One Saturday morning, Cath phoned to say, "Wooly and Mitt are going to see Betty Grable and John Payne this aft'. Want to go?"

"Sure, but I can't. I'm broke."

"Who isn't? I'll get Bertie to get his wagon and we'll be right up."

A short while later, she was ringing my front doorbell. I went out with my supply of empty soft drink and milk bottles, and other containers. Since the war began, Steinberg's grocery was paying 2¢ each for empty egg cartons, peach baskets, and Parisien Javal water bottles.

Cath and her brother Bertie waited at the foot of my steps, Cath standing somewhat removed from Bertie and his wagon, her face averted, as if she weren't really with him. In his wagon was her supply of empties.

"This is so embarrassing!" she hissed through gritted teeth.

"What it boils down to is, is it worth doing all this to see a movie or not?" I said. " — And the answer is yes, so let's get it over with."

We rattled up the street a few paces behind Bertie. When we reached Steinberg's, we took the stuff inside, collected our refunds, and made a fast exit.

Now that we had the money, we had another task ahead of us, that of persuading two teenagers of our acquaintance to collude with us in committing a Federal offence, by lending us their Registration cards.

After we secured the cards, we had to do our hair. Finally, with borrowed Regristration cards, the correct change, our hair in Betty Grable upsweeps, and wearing our older sister's or mother's high heels, Cath, Mitt, Wooly and I tottered up to the ticket wicket. The cashier didn't fall down laughing, which was sometimes the case, so we were let in.

We had become adept at flashing borrowed Registration cards. We knew how to present them to squinting cashiers: turned around so they had to read them upsidedown, then if requested to turn it the right way, with our thumb covering the date of birth of the person we'd borrowed it from. We were sometimes palming cards belonging to our mothers or great aunts. We had perfected this art before Registration cards came in, when we had borrowed 16 year olds' Student Streetcar Passes in order to "prove" we were sixteen. The trouble with those was that they bore the lender's picture, so you had to fix your hair to match the picture on the pass, no easy task when the lender had short hair and yours was long, or vice versa. We presented those with our thumb over the face.

If the cashier seemed to be scrutinizing the card too closely, we conducted diversionary feints. One of us would drop our purse, or our books, or our money, and another, with a better card, would offer to pay for her, while the others stooped to retrieve what had been dropped. Then we'd swarm past the ticket taker at the door in a bewildering blur.

Once Mitt observed with exasperation, "for heavens sakes, you can get *married* in this Province at the age of 14, but you can't see a movie till you're 16. A 14 year old married couple could be turned away from a movie in Montreal, then go home and play with their baby."

The movie law that you had to be 16 to get into the movie theatres stemmed not from the movies' content, but from a Montreal theatre fire in 1927 that claimed the lives of 77 children. We were in no danger of being corrupted by the movies we saw.

The most risqué remark I ever heard was in a movie called "My Son, My Son", with Madeleine Carroll and Brian Aherne. When the son was being born, the father, Brian Aherne, asked the midwife, "Is there anything I can do?" and the midwife glared at him and said, "You've done enough." There were raucous guffaws in the Empress Theatre at such a blatant allusion to you-know-what, and Cath gave me an elbow dig that said, "Get it?"

In the movie, "Kitty Foyle", made from the Christopher Morley novel about the quintessential "White Collar Girl", played by Ginger Rogers, there was a romantic scene where Kitty and Wyn, played by Dennis Morgan, were in Wyn's cabin in the Pocono mountains, in front of a fireplace, tapping out soundless tunes on each other's hands and foreheads. She's his secretary, and he's the publisher of a Philadelphia magazine. In the book, Wyn's original proposition to her had been, "Kitty, we've put the magazine to bed, why don't we go to bed ourselves?" But of course he wasn't allowed to say a thing like that in a movie. Instead, as she sat on the floor, he lay on the couch and read to her Tennyson's "The Lady of Shalott".

The language in films was salt-free as well. After David O. Selznick's 1939 victory in his battle to have Clark Gable say the word "damn" in "Gone With The Wind", controversy raged again in 1942 concerning certain words used by the sailors in Noel Coward's "In Which We Serve". The Hays office in the U.S. wouldn't allow the destroyer's captain, patterned on Lord Louis Mountbatten, to praise the crew after a bloody battle by telling them they'd done "damn well".

The movie we were seeing that day was a backstage musical, a genre that was one of our favorites. For some time we had made note of the clichés shared by MGM and 20th Century Fox musicals about vaudeville teams.

These musicals generally followed the established Comedia dell' Arte tradition of The Young Male Lover, The Young Female Lover, The Male Lover's Best Friend, The Dumb Clown, and The Female Lover's Servant or Best Friend, The Female Clown.

One classic situation would be where the team is on stage doing its number, and out front is Oscar Hammerstein the 1st, the famous impresario, who, if these musicals were to be believed, spent every waking moment in sleazy third-rate vaudeville houses, looking for acts. We recognized him right away by his Van Dyke beard, Chesterfield coat, opera hat, and cigar. (Sometimes the impresario would be Florenz Ziegfield, replete in top hat and tails). Classy dressers, these impresarios.

Hammerstein goes backstage after their performances and asks the girl to star in his upcoming show. She says she'll only go if her partner (whom she loves) gets to go too. The partner, (who loves her) knows perfectly well that Oscar Hammerstein the 1st isn't the least bit interested in him, so he picks a fight with her to make it easier for her to break away. She thinks he no longer cares, and takes the job.

73

On opening night, she's on the stage singing her very heart out and scanning the house for her former partner, but to no avail. What she doesn't know, is that he is standing in the wings with a hole in his hat and blear in his eyes — so much blear, in fact, that he can't see Oscar Hammerstein the 1st sitting out front — which is probably just as well.

In the movie musicals with contemporary settings, the heroine's best friend was often her secretary. She wore wide-shouldered suits and had a wise-cracking trenchant mouth, but a heart of moosh, and was always admonishing the heroine to, "Aw, give the big lug another chance," or, "Stop crying honey. You don't want him to see you like this."

Some notable best friends were Eve Arden, Kay Francis, Ilka Chase, and Rosalind Russell, until she became such a big star that she had a best friend of her own.

Often the best friend wore her hair in a bun, and horn-rimmed glasses on her nose at the beginning of the movie, and in the last scene she removed her glasses and took the pins out of her hair, and right away she had a good figure.

The hero's best friend would fall down a lot, upset tables in nightclubs, get his foot caught in wastebaskets, slip fully clothed into swimming pools, and do double-takes. Red Skelton, Eddie Bracken, Phil Silvers, and Jack Carson all played best friends, often winding up at the end of the picture with the heroine's best friend — after she'd taken off her glasses and removed the pins from her hair.

Then there were the musicals about the girl who hopes to make it on the supper club circuit. In order to show that her act is going over big, you see a customer slowly lowering his fork and leaving his food untouched while he listens. A couple of diners exchange significant nods; and the waiters and bartenders pause in their labors, nudge one another, fold their arms, and nod in the direction of the singer, when anyone asks for a drink.

Should we have to leave our seats for any reason, we never felt that we would lose the storyline. All we had to do on our return was ask, "Has Oscar Hammerstein the 1st shown up yet?" or, "Have the waiters stopped serving?"

Another thing that happened in musicals was the singer always knew a song as soon as she glanced at the sheet music. Betty Grable was a past-mistress at this. She would be doing her act, and Oscar Hammerstein the 1st is in the audience, natch, and he hands her a piece of unpublished music which she takes a fast look at, goes, "Da-da-da", then breaks into song, complete with orchestration and choreography.

The movie we saw that day followed the regular pattern. John Payne wanted to marry Betty Grable, who was his dancing partner, and open a show in New York. But they had a fight, and she went off to Lake Louise in the Canadian Rockies for a dancing engagement with Cesar Romero. Carmen Miranda was John Payne's secretary, and went shopping for what she called "kneeck-knocks", which she put on her hat. Jackie Gleason was John Payne's best friend, and I think this time it was Charlotte Greenwood who told Betty to stop crying. Harry James's band supplied the music.

We emerged from the theatre agreeing that what we'd had to go through in order to see the movie had been worth it. Vivacious Betty had out-Grabled herself.

SAILORS OBSERVE YULE ABOARD SHIP

Hidden Dangers of Sea Fail To Dampen Merchant Seamen's Spirit

---

UNITE FOR HAPPINESS

Dinner Served in Two Shifts With Battered Old Gramaphone Supplying Christmas Music

---

For Canadians at home, Christmas this year will be much the same as formerly a time of pleasant relaxation, of cheerfulness and goodwill, when, for a brief moment, the cares of ordinary life are thrust aside by the aura of happiness and fun surrounding the occasion. No one would have it differently, for that is what Christmas should be, but this year more than ever, thoughts will turn to the thousands of Canadians who must make the best of Christmas away from home, fighting perhaps, or surrounded by constant danger at sea.

Perhaps the hardest lot of all is that of the men of the Merchant Navy, whom Christmas finds in their gray ships on the cold, heaving waters of the north Atlantic. These men are never relieved from the terrific strain of not knowing what dangers are hidden in the unrevealing sea about them, and when death may strike. Christmas in these surroundings can be very little different from any other day, but every-one from the captain down, and particularly the steward, co-operates to make it as cheerful an occasion as possible.

Eight bells; eight o'clock on Christmas morning, and the watch changes. Only the men required to keep the ship moving toward her destination go on duty, while the rest have a holiday until their turn on watch comes around.

Down below, in the throbbing, steamy atmosphere of the engine room and the dusty clamor in front of the boilers, the firemen and engine crew go about their tasks of keeping the heart of the ship constantly running. They are at least warm, but the heat is oppressive and stifling. In addition to their discomfort, these men are under a particular nervous tension, for they receive no warning of a submarine attack until the first depth charge detonates, with a crash as if the bottom of the ship had been struck with a mighty hammer. Sometimes there is no warning until the ship's side is ripped open by the rending blast of a torpedo. Then the chances of climbing the several flights of steeply pitched, reeling ladder to the comparative safety of the lifeboats are slim indeed, with three boilers of high pressure steam ready to burst when the sea water reaches the fires. Even safely away in the boats, the "black gang" suffers most from the effects of exposure and are the first to succumb. For the men on duty below decks there is little reminder of Christmas and never a moment's relief from their constant dread.

DINNER SERVED IN SHIFTS.

At mid-day the watch is broken and Christmas dinner is served to the men in two shifts, the first group sitting down at 11.20 and the next at noon. If the ship has been long at sea, the men are unlucky, for in that case fresh food supplies are exhausted, but otherwise the steward does his utmost in the creation of a feast for the occasion. There is plenty of roast turkey with cranberry sauce and vegetables to follow bowls of hot soup, and the meal is topped off with some special dessert. The table is appropriately decorated and abundant dishes of candy and nuts are placed about the mess.

CHAPTER TWELVE

ADIEU TO '42

For New Year's Eve of 1942, Cath, Wooly, Mitt, and I were all invited to the same dance. This did not come about by accident.

At the beginning of the school year, Cath and I met two boys named Tommy and Alan at a football game between Catholic High and D'Arcy McGee. We doubledated together a few times, then Cath had a Hallowe'en party.

After the other guests had left, Cath and Alan; Mitt and her date, Stan; and Wooly and her date, Paul, and Tommy and I sat in front of the fire, talking.

It was after midnight, and Wooly said, "Well, Hallowe'en's over. It's November.

"Is it November *already*?" Mitt said in this amazed tone. (Wooly told her later that she over-acted).

Cath and I recited in unison:
"Thirty days hath Septobre,
April, June and no wonder.
All the rest have peanut butter
Except Pasadena, which has the Rosebowl."
"The next thing you know it'll be Christmas," said Wooly.

" — and then New Year's," said Cath.

And that's how come we started talking about New Year's Eve.

Someone happened to mention there was a New Year's Eve dance at the YMCA in N.D.G., and Paul asked Wooly to go to it, then Stan asked Mitt; Alan asked Cath, and Tommy asked me.

As it was All Hallow's Eve, we must have cast a spell over them, because they had done just what we had wanted them to do.

On the big night, Tommy had to pick me up at Kresge's, where I was taking inventory. I'd been working there during Christmas vacation. It was on Sherbrooke Street, just around the corner from my home, and the pay was 25¢ an hour.

As I stood behind the ribbon counter, I had been able to listen to the records from the record department playing all day long. Bing Crosby had a new one out called "I'm Dreaming Of A White Christmas" that they kept playing because it put people in the Christmas spirit. Then there were other war ballads like "There'll Be Bluebirds Over The White Cliffs of Dover". As well, there were rousing war songs like "Praise The Lord And Pass The Ammunition"; and a novelty number called "Der Fuehrer's Face", which gave Hitler the Bronx cheer; and Glenn Miller's lively "Don't Sit Under The Apple Tree With Anyone Else But Me". My all time favorite war song title was written by a musician named Wingy Manone — "Stop The War, Them Cats is Killing Themselves".

The store manager's name was Mr. Pryor, and all the girls in the store had a crush on him. He was the only man working in the store. I guess all the girls would have had a crush on King Kong if he were the only male working in the store.

On Christmas Eve I got a dollar bonus in a Christmassy envelope with an oval cut out of it for the King's face to show through, with holly leaves wreathing the oval. I was stunned to get paid for four hours work I hadn't done, so when they asked me to work on the inventory on New Year's Eve, how could I refuse? (Besides, it gave me the chance to have Mr. Pryor see me all dressed up).

In any case, my working didn't interfere with the evening. Tommy picked me up at the store at 9, and we walked back to Cath's, where everyone was meeting, and took cabs up to the dance.

The orchestra was called The Modernaires, which also happened to be the name of the singing group that sang with the Glenn Miller orchestra. It played all the Miller hits such as "Chattanooga Choo-Choo" and "I know Why" — songs that had been featured in the Glenn Miller movies.

Our favorite Miller movie was "Orchestra Wives" — the story of the Miller band travelling on the road doing one night stands, and the strain such work placed on their personal lives.

Cath, Mitt, Wooly, and I had fallen in love with George Montgomery, who played the part of the cornet player in the Miller band. (The cornet was actually being played by Bobby Hackett, so we should have fallen in love with him). Ann Rutherford was as "sent" by his music as we were and fell in love with George Montgomery in the film. (Singer Dinah Shore, I read in a movie magazine of the time, fell in love with George Montgomery when she saw "Orchestra Wives" too. The difference was that she married him.)

Perhaps it was the influence of that movie, but as I danced with Tommy, I couldn't help noticing how cute the band's drummer was. He had curly hair and an easy smile, and played drums with assurance and taste. We made eye contact several times, which wasn't easy when one person is jitterbugging, and the other, drumming.

During intermission, Mitt, Wooly, Cath, and I went to the ladies room. As we renewed our lipstick and powdered our noses, we chattered excitedly.

"Isn't the band great?"

"Terrific."

"I like the drummer."

"Ya, he's cute."

"I'd love to meet him."

"Let's get their autographs."

"What? Don't be dumb. They're not famous."

"I know, but it would be a way of getting to speak to them."

"We don't have any paper."

When we came out into the lobby, we saw a table with some bridge score pads and small pencils on it. Someone picked up one of the pads, tore a few sheets off it, then picked up some pencils, and we returned to the hall.

Lucky for us, our dates were talking music with some of the band members in front of the bandstand, and when we girls approached the group, we brandished our papers and asked the musicians to sign them. They looked at us as if we were mad. We said, "You may be famous some day, and we want to be the first to have your autographs," so they goodnaturedly complied. I looked at the paper when the drummer returned it to me and saw that his name was Bob Peate.

"Who's your favorite drummer?" I asked him, "Gene Krupa or Buddy Rich?"

He laughed. "You say that as if there were only two drummers to choose from. I think Buddy Rich is a better technician, but Krupa is a more musical drummer. But there are a lot of other great drummers besides them: Sid Catlett and Cozy Cole; Jo Jones, with Count Basie — he knocks me out the way he plays with his sticks on his high hat. Then there's Nick Fatool; and Sonny Greer, with Duke Ellington."

I had obviously pressed the right conversational button. (Gloria, my grammar school mentor, would have been proud of me.)

"Ellington's coming to the Forum on Tuesday," he said.

"I know. I'm going with Tommy," I said, indicating my date, who played clarinet, and was engrossed in conversation with the band's clarinetist.

"Have you heard Tony Pastor's 'Paradiddle Joe'?" I asked.

He nodded. "The drummer on that is John Morris. He's good too."

"What is a paradiddle, anyway?"

"Come up on the stand and I'll show you." He gave me a hand up onto the stage, sat on the drummer's throne, picked up the sticks and demonstrated. Then he showed me a "flam", "rimshot", and a "ratamacue".

I shook my head in admiration. I was so engrossed while watching the speed of the sticks, that I leaned against his tom-tom and almost knocked it off its stand. I quickly righted it, and noticed a sticker on the drum that read, "Peate Musical Company".

"Hey", I said, "Peate Musical. Is that any relation to you?"

"It's my father's business."

Peate's, a music store and school on Mansfield Street in downtown Montreal, was known to every Montrealer who was interested in music.

The huge sign in the form of a bass viol in front of the Peate building was a Montreal landmark.

"I've been working there since high school," he said, "When I turn 19 I'm going to join the Air Force and become a pilot.

A drummer who flew a plane. That sounded glamourous to me.

"Do you go steady with him?" he asked, indicating Tommy.

I hesitated. While neither Tommy nor I had ever formally declared ourselves to be "going steady" with each other, he was, in fact, the only boy I had been going out with lately.

"No," I said.

"Could I call you sometime?"

"Yes," I said.

"What's your number?"

80

I was glad it was an easy one to remember. "ELwood 7744."

"ELwood 7744," he repeated, "I'll remember that."

It looked like the intermission was over. The musicians were coming back onto the bandstand and I rejoined Tommy on the dance floor. When the music resumed, as Tommy and I did the Lindy, Bob and I traded smiles. I couldn't help feeling a little like Ann Rutherford, in "Orchestra Wives".

*

Bob did remember the number, and phoned on the afternoon of January 1st to ask me to a movie that night. I couldn't go because I was going out to dinner with my parents, and afterwards to see Lana Turner and Clark Gable in a movie called "Somewhere I'll Find You" in which they played a couple of war correspondents. It was a particularly poignant film because it had been during the making of it that Gable's wife , Carole Lombard, had died in a plane crash while en route home from a war bond selling tour. And the movie added to my lore of the glamourous lives led by foreign correspondents.

We went out together the following night.

When we walked down my front walk together, I turned left to walk up the street, but he guided me to the right, to where his car was parked. He was the first boy I'd gone out with who had his own car. It wasn't a jalopy either, like in Andy Hardy movies. It was a Ford, bought just before new cars disappeared for the duration.

We drove downtown to see "Give Out Sisters", with the Andrew Sisters — a good frothy confection for a first date. We talked a bit going to and from the movie, but there wasn't time to find out much about one another. When we drew up at my front door, he asked, "Do you have to go in right away?"

As I'd never been out with a boy in a car before, I wasn't sure of the procedure.

"I guess not," I said, and leaned back against the seat. It was time to get to know each other. He was a much quieter type than I, so it looked as if it was going to be up to me to draw him out.

"You said you were going into the Air Force when you turn 19. When's your birthday?"

"May 4th."

"May 4th? That's a coincidence; mine's May 13th," I said. "We were both born under the sign of the bull. That means we're both stubborn. Know who else was born on May 13th? Daphne du Maurier. You know, she wrote *Rebecca*. And Joe Louis, my favorite boxer."

"Are you a fight fan?"

"Well I always liked to listen to the fights on the radio. I loved Clem McCarthy." I tried to imitate sports announcer Clem McCarthy's gravelly voice.

Then we talked about our families and discovered more coincidences. We were both the youngest; our mothers were both in their forties when we were born; and his sister and my brother Choate were both born on the same day of the same year.

When I told him my father worked for *The Montreal Star*, he said, "So does my uncle Hugh."

"He *does*? My father's in the Art Department," I said.

"My uncle Hugh is General Manager," he said. "He's an Army Colonel, and right now he's Commanding Officer of the Royal Montreal Regiment. His full name is Hugh Graham Brewer. He was named after his uncle Hugh Graham, who founded The Star. Have you ever heard of Lord Atholstan?"

"Sure, my father often mentioned him."

"Well he was *my* uncle's uncle."

"For heaven's sake." This was getting spooky. Or, as Wooly, who liked making puns, would say, it was like a house without a bathrooom — uncanny.

Then we told each other about our friends. I told him about Cath, Mitt, and Wooly, and he told me about the boys he palled around with, Ian, Ian, and Bob.

He said he and his friends hung out at Sol's Soda Fountain on the corner of Sherbrooke and Grosvenor, and I told him we hung out at Heller's on Sherbrooke near Marcil.

He told me they often went back to his place afterwards to play records and drums in the soundproof music room he had in his basement.

"We had it soundproofed so the noise wouldn't disturb my father. He's sick in bed on the top floor with heart trouble, and he's in an oxygen tent most of the time."

"That's too bad. It must be hard."

"It's especially tough for my mother. My brother and sister are both married and have homes of their own. I guess it will be even tougher on her when I go into the Air Force."

"Who's going to look after Peate's when you're in the Air Force?"

82

"My brother will," he said, "He's married with kids, so he won't be called up. He'll keep it going, and I'll go into the business when I get back."

"It's really sad about your father."

He nodded. "Especially when he was such an active person. We have a house on a lake in the Adirondacks, and he used to take every summer off so we could fish, boat, swim, hike, and shoot."

Then he told me that when his father was a teenager, he had toured Europe, the States, and Canada giving mandolin concerts. And though his family owned a music store in Utica, New York, he decided to settle in Montreal, when he was 19 and start his own music school and store. That had been in 1899.

"Mandolins may sound square and corny to you now, but they used to be really popular," Bob said. "It's funny how there are fashions in musical instruments, almost like there are in clothes. Mandolins were the big craze before and during the last war, and my father used to teach and conduct mandolin orchestras all over Montreal, at McGill, Loyola, the M.A.A.A. the Shamrock Club — all over the place. Then after the war, a Hawaiian music craze hit Montreal, and Hawaiian guitars sold like crazy. My father was in a Hawaiian group then that recorded for R.C.A. Victor."

I was impressed.

"Yeah, but when his group played in hotels and at weddings and dances," Bob went on, "They were treated like lowlife because they were musicians. They had to use the rear entrance to the building they were playing in; and they weren't always paid what they'd been promised. So Dad and some other musicians got together and formed the Musicians Guild of Montreal. Now musicians are treated better."

Then we started talking about music we liked, and he mentioned that every couple of months he and his friends drove down to New York City to hear the big bands, mostly in movie theatres.

"That sounds like fun," I said, envious.

"Yeah, it's a really good deal," he said. "At the Paramount, for instance, you can see a new movie, a stage show with a big band like Tommy Dorsey, Gene Krupa, or Benny Goodman, say, and a top singer like Anita O'Day or like now, Frank Sinatra. Then there's always a good comedian, and some kind of specialty act like Louis Jordan and His Tympany Five, and if you get there before one, it costs 40¢. Even if you go after one, it's still under a dollar. We usually go to two or three different theatres in a day."

"Sounds super," I said. "Did you hear about Frank Sinatra's opening at the Paramount the other night — when all the girls in the audience screamed when he came out on the stage, and became hysterical when he started to sing?"

"Yes," he said, "It must've been a publicity stunt."

"No, it wasn't. I would've done the same thing if I'd been there."

"You would have?" He seemed surprised.

"Sure." It was easy for me to identify with the girls in the audience who were incited to shriek and swoon merely by his prolonging a note or lingering over a musical phrase.

The car was cold, and his arm had found its way from the top of the seat to my shoulders. My collar was turned up against the cold, but I was shivering. He turned the motor on for a few minutes every now and then so he could put on the heater to warm it up, but it didn't stay warm long.

"Guess I'd better go in," I said.

As we walked up my front steps he said, "I'll be phoning you." He didn't ask if he could kiss me goodnight, so I was spared the necessity of having to say, "Not on our first date," à la dictates of the Sub Deb page in *The Ladies' Home Journal*. But who knows? Maybe I would have said yes.

The next day I woke up with a bad cold that I must have caught from sitting in the cold car for such a long time, and had to stay in bed. The worst of it was that when Tommy called to discuss what time he should pick me up for the Duke Ellington dance, I had to tell him I couldn't go. Bitter pill! The first name band I would ever have danced to, and one of my favorites, besides.

I begged and pleaded with my mother to let me go, but she was adamant. (Adamant Eve, as Wooly would say). "There'll be plenty of dances," she predicted, unsympathetically.

"How do you *know*?" I wailed.

"I know," she said. And there were. Every Saturday night — at Victoria Hall, the stately, stone-turreted building on Sherbrooke Street in Westmount, where we danced to Johnny Holmes's band; and every Friday night at high schools and YMCA's, where Bob played drums in a band called " The Serenaders", with Oscar Peterson on piano, and Maynard Ferguson on trumpet, and I went along to listen. As I sat on the straight-backed chairs that lined the walls of the gym of the N.D.G. Y, I discovered, to paraphrase Milton, that "they also swing who only sit and wait."

*

All through the winter and early spring of 1943, we girls in our Sloppy Joe sweaters and bobby-sox were the subject of newspaper editorials, radio panel discussions, psychologist and sociologist interviews, music critics' columns, and the conversation of hand-wringing parents.

The psychologists diagnosed us as suffering from mass hypnotism, mass hysteria, "mass frustrated love without direction", and a "repressed maternal instinct".

All this because we were Sinatra fans.

We were particularly put off by the snide magazine articles written about him, and by the psychologists who analysed us Sinatra fans in print, saying such things as his popularity was a manifestation of "wartime degeneracy", and we were no better than Holy Rollers. (The Holy Rollers must've been pleased.)

Since February, Sinatra had been the vocalist on "Your Hit Parade" on the radio every Saturday night, but because the recording musicians were on strike, he couldn't cut any new records. The end result was that many of the records he had made while singing with Harry James and Tommy Dorsey were reissued. His recording of "All Or Nothing At All" that he'd made with Harry James in 1939 was reissued in May of 1943. Cath and I swooned, drooled, and plotzed over it.

Teenage boys were jealous of their girlfriends' interest in Frank Sinatra, idiotically enough. (Bob called him 'that stringbean'). What did he think? — that there was a likelihood of my running off with him? How silly could he get? My chances of meeting Sinatra were as slim as he was — and yet — supposing somehow I got to New York when he was singing at the Paramount — say I won an essay contest like Gloria Jean did in "The Underpup" — and I went off to the Waldorf Astoria, where he always stayed when he played the Paramount — and I found out his room number, then took the elevator up to his floor, and knocked on his door.

When he called from the other side of the door, "Who is it?" I'd call back, "Maid!" and he'd open the door and — well, he was married of course, and he had the sweetest little girl, and I certainly wouldn't want to break up his marriage or anything, but perhaps we might just look at each other, and for one fine, careless, rapturous moment, that would have to last us both a lifetime, he'd gaze into my eyes and sing: "All, Or Nothing At All....."

OSCAR PETERSON is featured as piano soloist with Johnny Holmes Orchestra in a new series of weekly Sunday afternoon and evening dances at Chez Maurice Danceland, scheduled to start this Sunday.

Dorsey at Forum

Tommy Dorsey and his famous orchestra will be seen and heard at The Forum this evening in a show and dance session, the program beginning at 8.30 p.m. This outstanding orchestra is a favorite with both "sweet" and "swing" fans alike and its best-selling recordings number in the hundreds.

Bob playing drums with the Johnny Holmes orchestra.

CHAPTER THIRTEEN

MAGAZINES WE BELIEVED IN

.Cath often called on me after school on her way to the grocery store. I went with her, and on the way back we dropped into Meyer's Candy Store and bought a magazine, paying for it with Cath's mother's change. Then we went back to Cath's and read the magazine from cover to cover.

We were thorough magazine readers. While we didn't read the articles with titles like KNOW YOUR JAR LIDS, we absorbed just about everything else, from the ads to the stories and illustrations. Indeed, it was the illustrations that induced us to read the stories, especially the work of easel artists Coby Whitmore, Al Parker, and Jon Whitcomb. In addition to illustrating stories, they did magazine covers and ads. The girls they drew were pug-nosed, rosebud-lipped, and star-eyed. Sometimes Jon Whitcomb actually painted little stars in their pupils. He drew the first of the series of ads for Community Silverplate called BACK HOME FOR KEEPS which Cath and I collected. When Whitcomb joined the Navy, he was replaced by an artist who signed himself Michael. Their pictures were romantic depictions of servicemen returning home to their young wives.

Our favorite illustrator, however, was Irving Nurick. He was the artist who illustrated a series of Kotex ads called, ARE YOU IN THE

KNOW? His drawings of teenage girls were so accurate that we had the feeling he was following us around, sketching us. While Jon Whitcomb's girls' looks were unattainable, Irving Nurick's teenaged girls were easy for us to identify with; they looked just like us.

Cath and I perused the Kotex ARE YOU IN THE KNOW ads carefully, hoping to learn something. They consisted of etiquette and dating questions and multiple choice answers, such as:

IF HE STOOD YOU UP LAST NIGHT —

Should you blow your top

Be a tearful earful

Bide your time

Answer: Bide your time 'til he calls again, then give him the brush off.

When Cath and I had need for the product itself, we prevailed upon her brother Bertie to buy it for us. After all, we couldn't very well go into the drug store and buy it from the same man who had given us free samples of coughdrops when we were little girls.

He always wrapped the box in plain brown paper before giving it to Bertie, who handed it to us outside the store. We were prepared, while carrying it home, to tell anyone we might meet who chanced to ask, that it was cornflakes.

In addition to the Kotex ads, Irving Nurick also illustrated a page in *The Ladies' Home Journal* every month for teenage girls, called "The Sub Deb".

Written by Elizabeth Woodward, and later by Maureen Daly, it consisted of advice on the latest fashion fads; how to get along with your peers; and how to act with and toward boys — like, for instance, not to allow him to kiss you goodnight on the first date.

We perhaps put too much stock in the advice on "The Sub Deb" page.

In one of the previous summer's issues, the Sub Deb columnist advised that a girl should keep her ear to the ground, and if it looked as if her boyfriend was going to dump her, she should give him the brush-off first, to save face. (If you have your ear to the ground, you should do something to save face.) One of the clues she said to look for was if he began saying nice things about other girls.

When I read that, I immediately thought of how often Jack, the boy I liked best at the time, had mentioned that Wooly looked like Rita Hayworth. Wooly *should* have looked like Rita Hayworth; she spent every waking moment trying to. Nevertheless, after reading that column, the next time I saw Jack, while we were going for a walk, which was all we ever did, I told him I didn't want to see him again. He came to a skidding stop and looked surprised, but didn't ask why, and I didn't volunteer an explanation. I guess I'd expected him to protest and plead his case the way they did in magazine stories and movies, but teenage boys don't behave that way in real life, and teenage girls don't know that. In any case, he stopped phoning me. The funny thing was that he never phoned Wooly either. For all I know, he may have read an advice column for boys, suggesting that one way to please a girl is to say nice things about her friends.

But ads and advice columns aside, what we really bought the magazine for, were the short stories.

Once the United Stated entered the war, we noticed that magazine short fiction shared certain similarities.

If the protagonist wasn't in any branch of the Armed Services, it was explained why in the first paragraphs. Generally it was due to a trick knee he had sustained during a football game. That was supposed to make him sound more appealing than if he suffered from other problems that also rendered one 4F, such as flat feet, a double hernia, myopia, a murmuring heart, a punctured eardrum, or having to support one's widowed mother.

Thus, the average story started something like this:

As he waited for Rosa, Jim glanced at the two sailors standing at the bus stop on the opposite corner, and silently cursed his trick knee.

"If only I could be out there with them on the high seas, giving it to those Nips," he muttered under his breath.

Just then, a man dressed in the uniform of the Army Air Corps, came out of the drug store.

"If I could only be up there with those boys flying over Tokyo," Jim murmured, averting his head in shame as the man passed.

He had been the hero of the football game that crisp fall afternoon, with the scent of apples and burning leaves in the air, when, while running for a touchdown, Krasnowski had brought him down on the five yard line.

After the doctor had examined the injury done to his leg, he rested his hand lightly on Jim's shoulder and shook his head sadly, "I'm afraid you'll have a trick knee for the rest of your life, m'boy," said he, "If there's ever a war, you'll never be able to serve."

Jim wondered now if that gain he'd made for his team was worth the guilt he felt every time he saw a serviceman in the uniform of his country.

Flipping his cigarette into the gutter, he spotted Rosa.

One time Faith Baldwin wrote a story for Collier's about a *girl* who hadn't joined the *women's* services because of a trick knee. (Faith Baldwin was very patriotic). She didn't say the girl's trick knee was the result of a football injury, but Cath and I speculated that the heroine could have been injured trying to dodge a forward pass, although Faith Baldwin didn't usually get that racy.

(We read too, in a movie magazine, that Paramount's new fair-haired boy, Sonny Tufts, wasn't in the armed forces due to a trick knee from football).

Other magazine writers we looked for were Rose Franken, of "Claudia" fame; Vera Caspary, whose classic, "Laura", ran in *Collier's* and our all-time favorite, Adela Rogers St. Johns. Among the male writers we sought out were Ernest Lehman, Mel Heimer, and Jack Finney.

Lesser writers than they, however, seemed to write to a given formula:

In the *Ladies' Home Journal*, the heroine and hero invariably "met cute". They usually lived in Greenwich Village or Manhattan, and the girl might do something like accidentally lock herself out of her apartment, while wearing only a towel. The hero is her new next door neighbor who finds her there. She's all embarrassed, and explains that she'd come out to get her newspaper or milk bottle, when a gust of wind had blown the door shut behind her. He gets the keys from the Super, opens the door with a flourish, and asks her for a date.

Or in a *Good Housekeeping* story, the girl might be a glamourous model that this photographer had always thought was too beautiful to ask to go out with him. Then one day she has a bad cold and has to stay home in bed. The hero then has to take something to her and he sees her with her nose all red and running, eyelids swollen, and a fever blister on her lip. This vision gives him the courage to ask her out.

Another type of story was about a poor girl who falls in love with a boy who she thinks is poor as well. Everything is fine between them until she finds out he isn't poor at all, but, (say not so!) rich. This discovery upsets her to the extent that she breaks off with him.

Cath and I had a certain amount of difficulty trying to follow that type of story.

"I don't get it. She doesn't like him because he's rich?"

"I guess so."

"What an idiot!"

"Turn the page."

Anyway, after a while, he does something that shows that even though rich, he still has some redeeming qualities, like, say, trick knee and all, he saves her little brother from drowning, and they get back together.

Sometimes that story was done in reverse, with the girl rich, and the boy poor. Then he says he'll only marry her if she'll agree to renounce her inheritance and live with him in a vine-covered hovel, speak in double negatives; eat high fat content hamburger; buy items marked "seconds" in factory outlets; and drive with him in his beat-up Chevy. And the girl lovingly consents to these provisos. (Those guys were sure different from the men that blues singer Alberta Hunter sang about, who "had a hand full of 'gimme' and a mouth full of 'much oblige' ".)

As all Chevies in these stories were described as "beat-up", we decided that maybe someone, antagonistic to Chevies, went around punching them out. Perhaps it was the same testy individual, who "hammered out" agreements at bargaining tables.

When we finished reading the magazine, we took it back to Mr. Meyer.

Looking him straight in the tieknot just above his apron bib, I said, "I didn't know it, Mr. Meyer, but my mother bought this same magazine downtown this afternoon." Then, for a ring of authenticity, I added, "She wanted something to read coming home on the streetcar."

As I recited this, Mr. Meyer looked straight ahead into space as if trying to compute the mathematical probabilities of such a coincidence occurring with the degree of frequency that I cited it, with the possible view of sending it to Ripley's Believe It Or Not column.

It was true that I did use that explanation quite often. After my speech, during which his lips seemed to move imperceptibly along with mine, he examined the magazine for fingerprints, found none — Cath and I were scrupulous about keeping it clean; in fact, if the pages got crumpled, we *ironed* them — stabbed at the NO SALE key on the cash register, and refunded Cath's mother's change.

It may not have been a very nice thing to do, conning Mr. Meyer that way, but what are you supposed to do when you salivate each time the latest issues of magazines appear on the stands, and you can't afford to buy them? Besides, how else would Cath and I have learned about life and love?

Are you in the know?

If he stood you up last night—

- ☐ Should you blow your top
- ☐ Be a tearful earful
- ☐ Bide your time

Tears or temper won't teach him. Bide your time 'til he calls again, then give out with the brush-off. Keeping calm wins many a victory . . .

CHAPTER FOURTEEN

THE WAR EFFORT (JUNIOR GRADE)

Cath opened her front door one afternoon in June of '43, rolled her eyes heavenward, and hissed, "She's on a patriotic rampage."

When I followed Cath into the kitchen I found her mother seated at the table reading *The Gazette*, and her brother Bertie reading a comic book.

"Hello Mary," Cath's mother greeted me, "And how's your father feeling?"

My father had been confined to bed since early February when he'd had a prostate operation.

"Still not very well, thanks. He doesn't seem to be getting any better. He's lost so much weight, and my mother has to give him eight 222's a day for the pain, so he's groggy most of the time."

"Eight 222's ? Glory be to God! It must be hard on your mother too."

"Yes, it is."

Cath's mother picked up the newspaper she had been reading and looked at me over her glasses. "You're just in time to hear about the scrap drive."

Oh goody! And to think that if I'd arrived five minutes later I would have missed it!

Cath's mother started reading aloud, "Today, Wednesday, and Friday, Montreal will see a campaign of considerable importance to the war effort — a drive by the Salvage Committee of the Montreal War Services Co-ordinating Council to bring out salvage of the hidden and forgotten variety, salvage that must be ferreted out from attics and cellars'." She looked up at us. "There you are, girls. Here's your chance to do your patriotic duty."

Oh, had we been looking for a chance to do our patriotic duty?

"You can start in the basement and put anything you see that would be suitable for the war effort to one side. Then I'll look it over, and Bertie can help you carry it upstairs and out to the curb."

Bertie looked up from his comic book as thrilled at the prospect as we were.

"Aw Ma," Cath protested, "Mary doesn't want to do that."

Cath's mother fixed me with a surprised look. "Mary doesn't want to help her country win the war?"

"It isn't that," Cath defended me. "Anyway I don't want to do it either."

Cath's mother went on reading. "It says here that all the stuff can be sold to war industries and used in the war effort. And the money the Salvage Committee gets will be used to entertain the troops."

A double-barreled incentive. Cath and I looked at one another. Well it *would* be good to do something for the troops.

We went down the cellar steps and looked around. What a bunch of stuff. There were piles of magazines, shelves full of empty jars, paint cans, brushes, brooms, rakes, hoses, tires, (though they never owned a car) — all kinds of stuff.

"Where should we start?" I asked Cath, feeling overwhelmed.

"Maybe over in the corner by the coal bin, and work our way to the middle of the room," she said.

We worked until suppertime. By the time we'd finished, the basement was tidy, and Cath's mother's sudden surge of patriotism was assuaged.

We were being told at every turn how young people could help the war effort. All kinds of public service ads were directed at kids, trying to appeal to their latent patriotism.

The Scott Paper Company showed how mothers could even enlist their *toddlers'* aid in helping them win the war.

While she did her housework and warwork, the little tyke was instructed how to wash up after play, make his own bed, and clean the table. His mother could send to the Scott company for a Clean-Up Warden Arm Band for him to wear while he worked.

The Tootsie Roll ads on the back of comic books featured The Tootsie Roll of Honor, showing boys and girls doing their bit for defence by raking their school grounds because the school's janitor was in the Navy; painting chairs for the U.S.O.'s Recreation House; and fixing their own school lunches.

The Royal Bank of Canada ads showed a 10 year old boy doing his post-war planning by buying a War Saving Stamp every week and pasting it in his book. And Christie's Biscuits ran a series in the newspapers called "How Young Canadians Can Help Win The War". Suggestions offered were: collecting books for the I.O.D.E. (Imperial Order of the Daughters of The Empire) to send to servicemen; and donating money to the Kinsmen's Milk for Britain Fund.

Also, in 1943, the Canadian Auxilliary Service Corps introduced a new Cadet Corps for girls 12 and over, which Cath and I figured was a result of our efforts.

Back in 1940 we had envied the boys who belonged to the Air Cadets — the junior version of the Royal Canadian Air Force. They got to wear natty Air Force blue uniforms with their own crest and insignia, and after school were given elementary training similar to the R.C.A.F., learning about aeroplane engines, aircraft recognition, map reading, model building, and other air lore. The Air Cadet League was headed up by Air Marshall Billy Bishop, the great World War One fighter pilot.

One day Cath and I got to wondering why they didn't have a branch of the Air Cadets for girls, so we decided to write Billy Bishop and suggest the idea to him. We spent a whole afternoon working on the letter and sent it to him care of The Department of National Defence in Ottawa.

We waited and waited for a reply, but none was forthcoming, so we figured he was either too busy with the war, or he hadn't received the letter.

But when news of the formation of the new Cadet Corps was released, we reckoned he had received our letter after all. In any case we took credit for the new Cadet Corps for girls, but didn't join it because by that time our only interest in a uniform was if there was a boy inside it.

*

Older teenagers made their own particular kinds of contributions. McGill students organized a "Mile of Coppers" campaign to buy Bren guns for the Canadian Army. Several lines of pennies were set out on the campus between the Roddick Gates and the tomb of James McGill.

The band Bob played in, The Serenaders, played a three night stand at the Snowdon Theatre. The show was produced by the students of Montreal High School in aid of that school's drive for another mobile canteen to send overseas. For that engagement, the band was rechristened Percy Ferguson and His Victory Serenaders.

"With Oscar Peterson on piano and Maynard Ferguson playing the trumpet," their advance press notice read, "the show is said to supply proof, if any were needed, that local high schools and colleges are a source of a wide variety of talent."

Some of the older teenage girls were junior hostesses at Air Force House on Sherbrooke St. They danced and talked with the airmen who were far from home, sometimes going out with them afterwards, or inviting them to their parents' house for a home-cooked meal.

Other older teenagers joined troop shows like the MRT Tin Hats, Hilda Galt's Dance for Defence, and The Evans Sisters Revue. They usually worked in offices by day, and travelled from camp to camp in busses in the evenings and on weekends, to entertain servicemen. Many a weary stenographer showed up at the office the day after a show with traces of stage make-up still evident.

*

Adults may have been more directly affected by rationing, shortages, and wage and price controls than we kids, but the effects of these impositions filtered down to our age group.

The hardest of all was the shortage of sweets. With sugar and butter rationed, it became more and more difficult to appease our sweet tooth. Coca-Cola ads apologized for Cokes being in short supply; ice cream makers were sorry they couldn't produce enough to go around; and eventually you couldn't even buy Wrigley's chewing gum, Life Savers, or Jell-O.

But the worst rationing burden to bear was the chocolate bar shortage. Cadbury's chocolate bar ads said: "Out of stock? Please try again. Much goes to our fighting men!" Neilson's chocolate bar ads begged our indulgence. Whitman's chocolate sampler ads told us that thousands of pounds of Whitman's chocolate went to the fighting fronts, but, "try again. Your dealer receives an allotment regularly."

In a pig's eye.

Cath and I developed a routine whereby we would go into Meyer's Candy Store every day, and if Meyer was busy with a customer, we would stand aside, pretending to be reading the magazine covers. When he was free, Cath would give him the dazzling smile she was capable of — the one that revealed all her teeth and had a bit of eye twinkle in it — and we'd say cheerily, "Hi, Mr. Meyer." Then I would lower my voice and ask confidentially, "Any chocolate bars today?" and the answer always came back, "Sorry."

But one great come-and-get-it day, Mr. Meyer leaned forward and whispered hoarsely in my ear, and I could feel his hot breath on my neck as he said, "I'm expecting a shipment in on the fourteenth."

Our hearts leapt. "You *are*?"

"Yes," he said, "but don't let it get around. And be here early."

"Oh we *will*, we *will*," we said, fair skipping out of the shop.

By the 12th or 13th we could contain ourselves no longer and went in to ask how the shipment was coming along. Meyer read us the bills of lading provocatively, and we listened with mouths watering and tastebuds tingling.

When the shipment day dawned, we sidled up to the counter, and, scarcely moving my lips, I asked, "Did the chocolate bars come in?"

"Yes," Meyer said, "Two to a customer."

I immediately dropped my Mata Hari demeanor and whined, "*Twoooo*? Is *that* all?"

"You're not the only ones waiting for them."

"I know, but *two....*"

"I'm saving them for good customers," he said.

Cath and I gasped in unison. We were *stung*. "But *we're* good customers," Cath protested, "We come here all the *time*."

Meyer's lip curled. "But do you *buy* anything?"

That gave us pause. It was true that we mostly went there to cash in bottles and read his magazines, but it hadn't occurred to us that he might not regard us as good customers.

"We'll take the two each then," Cath said, mollified, and the exchange of money for chocolate bars was surreptitiously made.

Outside the store, we looked at the bars. They weren't like any we'd seen before. They were in a powder blue wrapper, and the name was an unfamiliar wartime brand.

Cath started to read the ingredients listed on the wrapper, her voice rising with indignation: "Soybeans, artificial flavoring, artificial sweetening, artificial coloring, and artificial chocolate." She pulled off the offending paper and bit into the bar angrily.

"How is it?" I asked, knowing full-well the answer.

"If I had artificial choppers," she snarled, "I might like it."

*

Everyone had one particular shortage that affected him more than any other. In addition to the chocolate bar shortage, the other one that affected me was the disappearance of peanut butter.

Had I complained at the irony that just as I became old enough to wear nylons, they were no longer available? Not me. Nor did I say a word when the marketing of rubber heels was discontinued. And there wasn't a peep out of me when bobby pins faded into history. But no peanut butter? — The one food staple I had depended on all my life?

While for Scarlett O'Hara it took the hunger pains gnawing in her stomach to bring home the full impact of the Civil War as she stood in the barren cottonfields of Tara, shaking her fist at the heavens; for me it was the peanut butter shortage. I resolved that after the war, paraphrasing Scarlett, "As God is my witness, I'll never go without peanut butter again."

What affected my mother most was the scarcity of tea, because in our home, just as at the Mad Hatter's, it was "always tea time".

No matter how many cups of tea she brewed in a day — and there were many — she took each one seriously. Though her way may not have been as stately as *chanoyo*, the traditonal Japanese "art of tea", she went through a definite ritual nonetheless. And she was as philosophical about tea's curative powers as any Zen Abbot. So when the blow of tea rationing fell, it struck her hard. She didn't know how to cope, and was constantly running out of tea coupons, before her next allotment came. Then she hit upon a scheme.

"You'll just have to go up to Meyer's and buy me a cup of tea," she said.

"But it's against the law," I said.

Meyer's had a soda fountain where soft drinks, tea, and coffee were dispensed, but the law was, (after tea and coffee were rationed) that you couldn't buy it in a restaurant or lunch counter to take out. You had to drink it there. Don't ask me why. (A pox on the Wartime Prices and Trade Board).

98

"Isn't it enough that I have a son in the Army? Must I be deprived of my tea as well?" she said.

"But I could get arrested," I said.

"Oh, you don't have to worry about that; I'll tell you exactly what to do."

So, following my mother's instructions, I took an empty Crisco tin in a brown paper bag up to Meyer's and sat down at the counter.

Mr. Meyer looked surprised to see me sitting there and said, "So. Mary. What do you want?"

"I'd like a pot of tea, please." I said.

Another surprise for Mr. Meyer.

He switched the heat on under the kettle and placed a cup and saucer in front of me. When the water had boiled he poured some into a cup-sized metal teapot, and dropped a teabag into it.

"How much is that?" I asked.

"Ten cents. You want milk with it?"

"No thanks."

I put the dime on the counter, and when he was busy with another customer, dumped the contents of the teapot into the Crisco tin, put the lid in place, and took off fast to get it to my mother while it was still hot. Another reason for my haste was that for all I knew, one of the spies from the Wartime Prices and Trade Board could have been nipping at my heels. I felt like Eliza crossing the ice floes as I ran down the street with the tea sloshing around in the Crisco tin.

Mr. Meyer must've had another surprise when he saw how quickly I seemed to have drunk the scalding tea — straight from the pot — and that I appeared to have swallowed the teabag.

My mother was waiting for me at the front door and gratefully took the tin with the tea bag in it from my hands. Removing the teabag from the water, she said, "I can get two more cups out of this easily. Thank you, darling."

After that episode, I tried to keep her supplied with hot drinks and still remain within the law. I spotted an ad for something called Appletine Fruit Koffy, a pure apple product, and showed it to her.

"Coffee made of *apples*?" she said, "It sounds terrible. Besides, I don't like coffee."

"How about some nice hot Ovaltine?"

She averted her head.

"Hot cocoa?"

No thank you.

"What about a nice cup of hot Bovril or OXO?"

Not her cuppa.

One day I bought her something called Postem, which didn't require ration stamps. It tasted like a cross between tea and coffee. When I made her some, she took a sip, and quoted what I recognized from my collection of Abraham Lincoln one-liners: "If this is tea, give me coffee. If it's coffee, bring me tea."

The hardship that affected Bob the most was gasoline rationing. He was always running low on gas and had been the victim several times of a crime germane to the times: having gas syphoned from his gas tank.

He never managed to develop the philosophical attitude about it that was demonstrated in a Simpson's Department Store ad that shrugged:

"What if you can't get gas for your car? It's heaps more fun to hop on a bicycle and follow the country byways instead of the same old highways!...Or rediscover the thrill of hiking on our lovely Mount Royal, or the fun of tramping through the cool, green woods! A trip to our Sportswear Section will show you how decorative you can look and how downright comfortable you can feel when dressed for these pleasant jaunts!"

*

After the U.S. had entered the war, we were hounded with guilt-producing tips on how to spend our spare time and spare cash.

Cath's brother Bertie had a comic book called How Boys And Girls Can Help Win The War that we looked through one afternoon.

"Just look at the stuff American kids are expected to do." Cath said.

It was a staggering list.

They were encouraged to join such organizations as the Boy Scouts, which trained them as firefighters and messengers, in case of emergency; the Camp Fire Girls, who helped distribute posters and important announcements to stores and other public buildings; the Girl Scouts, who were equipped to serve as messengers and canteen helpers; 4H Clubs, whose members were trained to keep farm machinery in top working condition, and help neighboring farms in case of emergency; and the Junior Red Cross, whose speciality was knowing how to administer First Aid.

Tips were given as to how kids could earn money to buy War Savings Stamps which they were told they should ultimately convert to War Bonds. Such jobs as delivering groceries, caddying, selling

100

magazine and comic book subscriptions, cutting grass, running errands, shampooing dogs, and tending babies, were put forward.

In addition, the comic book cautioned against spreading rumors and troop information, and preached against racial intolerance. It also recommended that kids help free their parents for their war work. Hints in this regard were: washing dishes, keeping household items and bikes in good repair, and helping to preserve the family car and its tires, by walking.

They were also encouraged to learn about aircraft spotting, and should there be an air raid, were shown how to equip a "Refuge" room in their home, and how to look after their pets during such an eventuality.

Whew!

"Keep this out of sight," Cath cautioned Bertie. "If Ma sees it she might have another patriotic fit."

Alas, though Bertie could keep the comic book out of his mother's hands, we couldn't keep Cath's mother from reading the public prints. It was just about a week after the scrap drive when she struck again.

We were trapped in her kitchen as she started to read aloud from a newspaper, "Now is the time to obtain a suitable vacant lot for a Victory Garden."

Uh-oh.

"I have the perfect spot for a Victory Garden — right at the foot of the back steps. All it needs is for you girls and Bertie to dig it up."

Us girls?

"That earth's like cement out there," Cath protested.

"It will be fine once it's turned over."

"Do you expect us to dig that stuff?" Cath asked.

Us? Us? How did I get into this?

"It's our patriotic duty."

Our? Was she going to be digging too?

"By growing food in our backyard or in vacant lots we help out the farmer, who is overworked, and the people who ship and pack food as well."

That wasn't much of an incentive — helping some tired farmers and food packers. At least when we cleaned the basement we could picture some servicemen enjoying themselves because of our efforts.

Nevertheless, the following Saturday, Cath, Bertie, and I were out there with spades, and we attacked the hard-packed earth. Cath had been right; it *was* like cement. It took us hours, but eventually we managed to turn it over.

"Good," Cath's mother pronounced after inspecting it, "Now you just have to take a rake and break up the soil and remove the stones."

Just?

After that was done, Cath's mother bent down, picked up a handful of dirt, and looking like Luise Rainer in "The Good Earth", said, "Ah, there's nothing like the simple pleasure of feeling the earth run through your fingers."

Poetic.

Ah well, as the current song had it, we were "Doing It For Defence."

"Help win the war?...<u>ME</u>?"

Indeed yes, young lady...you and some eleven million other girls in this country of ours!

How? In all the countless ways that women always find.

The Red Cross wants you. Volunteer workers are wanted in civilian defense, in undermanned draft boards, in auxiliary services for men in uniform, in vital social service work. And things must be kept going at home, too, while the boys are away.

Help? You bet you can! And what a lift eleven million of you will give your Uncle Sam!

And if we may make the suggestion—*learn to type!* Making typewriters is our business, so we know how the door to opportunity swings open for the good typist. Ability to type, important always in peace times, is even more useful now. Twice-welcome is the girl who brings with her not only the will to serve, but the skill to save precious hours of working time.

And typing skill comes quickly to women's deft fingers —not the blazing speed of the expert, of course, but speed sufficient for most of our workaday world. A typewriter, a simple manual, a few days of faithful practice—and you're *twice* as able to help!

If you buy a typewriter, now or later, we hope you will consider machines bearing two names long famous in typewriter history—L C Smith (office) and Corona (portable). They may not be available everywhere today, as most of our output is for the defense program. But they're worth knowing about, and we will be glad to mail descriptive folders free on request.

SMITH-CORONA
OFFICE *Typewriters* PORTABLE

Montreal Star Nov. 24, 1943

14 **Theatres**

Tin Hats' New Revue

Production Numbers Are Highlights

MONTREAL is proud of its war work, in all its various phases, from knitting to fighting. Among these, this city has gained an enviable reputation for the quality and variety of the entertainment it offers Service folk in this district. One of the outstanding organizations in this department is The Montreal Repertory Theatre's "war baby," The Tin Hats troop show.

* * *

THE quality of the Tin Hats troop show has proved, particularly this last year, a bit of a boomerang. The training and experience gained with the unit has intrigued professional interest for years past; Tin Hatters are now radio, stage and cafe stars. But they have usually left singly- and replacement wasn't too difficult. This year, however, The Royal Canadian Navy's "Meet The Navy," took the three male comedians and a dozen of the girls from the show. So, last night, when The Tin Hats offered their new revue, with new members forming the bulk of the cast, loyal followers held their breaths and hoped.

* * *

THE hoping was a nice gesture, but quite unnecessary. And they didn't really need to hold their breaths. For the Tin Hats have recruited a new cast which is as rich and sparkling in its talents, in its own way, as the originals who made the troupe famous for most of four years. Introduced to each other little more than a month ago, they are still finding out new things about each other; their combinations and permutations of comedy and song aren't quite as blooming, yet, as they will be. Which means that Tin Hats fans have something rather special to look forward to, for their show last night was a definitely entertaining one.

* * *

THE production numbers were outstanding. In costumes, in routines, in settings, they were strikingly rich, attractively original. No complaints, incidentally, could be made about the way the costumes were mounted, either. Richest was the bolero, Norma Darling's creation, with Norma herself as the black-gowned centrepiece, lithe and gaze-making. For sparkling fun, "Elmer's Day on

Leave," with costumes of attractive simplicity and a theme that is catchy and bright, was memorable.

* * *

OF the soloists, the charming youth of Claire Ponman's work made her a standout; an ex-Tin Hats favorite, she is loaned to the show, this week, by the management of The Chateau Frontenac. Cortland McNeil, with his songs, his ukelele and his trunkful of excellent gags, gained the most chuckles in the show. The novel comedy interludes were handled by Frank Heron, Dave Campbell, Jack Simpson and Louis Mulligan with Eileen Clifford acting as the lovely lady, which chore she does so well and so appropriately. The pert little lady with the voice, amber-haired Babs Lee, did her solos in the production numbers. Joyce Webber, Art Prevost, Bill Taylor, contributed their talents to the musical items.

* * *

THE fashion show, of course, an important portion of "Modes for Morale," was right out of this world—out of a man's world, at any rate. Highlighted by the appearance of Harry Conover's famous cover girls, milady's fashion appetite was whetted to a famine point by the parade of gowns and stuff which were shown. It was a rich evening's entertainment. It will be repeated this evening. **ROY KERVIN.**

Montreal Star April 14, 1942

Heads Revue

Hilda Galt, director - producer of the popular troop show, the Hilda Galt Revue, which will be presented to the public for the first time tomorrow evening at Victoria Hall in aid of The Wings For Britain Fund.

Galt Revue Tomorrow

Fine Show Rehearses For Wings for Britain Benefit at Victoria Hall

THE Hilda Galt Revue which will be presented to the public for the first time tomorrow evening, at Victoria Hall, in aid of Wings For Britain, has, besides the features of dancing and singing and instrumentalists which have made it so popular with local troops, a number of new features to make it even richer. One of these will be the appearance, a special concession, of the R.C.A.F. Brass Band from No. 5 Manning Depot, Lachine. Another will be a surprise production number built around the song "Wings For Britain", by Elizabeth Douglas, which, incidentally, goes on sale at all music stands the same day, with total proceeds in aid of Wings For Britain. Jane Lee, popular favorite of theatregoers in all the capitals of the Empire, will be the vocalist.

* * *

FOR the rest, the show, rich in dancing talent, smartly costumed and excellently trained, will be seen in numbers ranging from ballet to boogie-woogie. The troops say the Galt Girls are as proficient in the one style as the other. A special compliment to Miss Galt's show is the fact that Ned Wayburn, famous dancing master, under whom Miss Galt studied, is making a special trip to Montreal to see the show.

Montreal Gazette May 26, 1944

Courtesy of *The Gazette*, Montreal

CHAPTER FIFTEEN

THE GINGERBREAD GIRL

Bob was sworn into the Air Force on June 28th, 1943, and reported to Manning Depot in Lachine, a suburb of Montreal.

A week later, he got the evening off, and arrived at my place after supper. It was the first time I'd seen him with his hair cut in a brush-cut, and in uniform. As all the boys did, he looked handsome. The uniform made him look older and more mature, although he had been more subdued and less lighthearted since his father's death from heart failure two months before.

The next day he was transferred to Toronto.

With Bob away, I figured I might as well continue going to school during the month of July. I was working towards the goal of receiving a typing diploma for being able to type 60 words a minute without making a mistake; and a shorthand diploma for taking shorthand at 80 words a minute. (Some of those politicians I'd be interviewing as a foreign correspondent might be fast talkers).

The school's summer hours were 9 to 1, and the principal gave my classmate, Becky, and me the opportunity of earning while learning. The Greek War Relief Fund had contacted him asking him to supply typists to work for them part-time.

Terrible things were happening in Greece. In Athens, starvation was killing 200 people a day. Only one child in ten was surviving the first weeks of life. The conquering Germans and Italians had left the people to die of hunger and disease. Little Greek children were fighting over garbage, and dying in alleyways and now Canadians were donating money to help the Red Cross feed them. The Greek War Relief Fund offices were in the Royal Bank Building on St. James Street. Our job was to send out receipts to the people who sent in donations. So many of the donations came from Canadians of Greek extraction and that, coupled with the fact that the average person's handwriting and signature isn't easy to decipher anyway, made our task more difficult. We exhausted such remarks as "It's Greek to me" and "The Greeks have a word for it" and "Beware of Greeks bearing gifts" on the first day.

One day in the third week I'd worked there, the boss came to my desk and said, "Will you come with me to the stockroom on the next floor? I need some help with the stationery supplies."

I rode up in the elevator with him, and he, (Mr. Manners!) got off the elevator ahead of me, and started down the hall. Just as I was about to step off the elevator, the elevator boy whispered to me, "Watch out for that guy. He's a bugger."

"He is?" I said, hesitated, then stepped back into the elevator.

"Wanna go back to the floor you got on at?"

"Uh — yes, " I said.

Down we went, and when I stepped off, I said, "Could you hold the elevator for me please?"

"Sure," he said, and I went back to my desk. Becky looked up from her typing when I said, "I'm going home."

"How come?" she asked as I reached into the desk drawer for my purse.

"The elevator boy said the boss is a wolf," I explained inadequately. Becky shrugged, and went on typing. I left the office and took the elevator to the lobby.

"Thanks for the warning," I said to the operator as I left. Walking towards my streetcar stop, I started feeling like a jerk. Maybe I'd over-reacted. Maybe all he'd really wanted me to do was to help him carry the stationery.

It had been the word "bugger" that had stopped me in my tracks. Not that I knew what it meant, or even if it had a meaning. All I knew was that it was a swear word, and people so seldom swore, that when they did, you paid attention. And the elevator operator must have been in a good position to know about the man. Maybe some of the other girls returning from the stockroom had complained to him or in front of him, about the boss. I wasn't wise in the ways of handling wolves, and I sure wasn't looking to learn by dealing with him.

There was an actress named Iris Adrian who defined the genre of the cheap blonde babe. She talked out of the side of her mouth and didn't take borscht from anyone, least of all some masher making a pass at her. Her standard line, uttered from the side of her mouth, was, "Lay off, Bud, or I'll call a cop." Maybe I could have used that line on the boss, but perhaps it wouldn't have been effective without the true Iris Adrian delivery.

As I waited for the streetcar, (a long wait in the middle of the afternoon in the financial district) the lines of a rhyme that my mother had read to me when I was a little kid ran through my head. It was from the story about a gingerbread man cookie that an old woman had baked, and when she opened the oven door, the gingerbread man jumped out and ran away, followed by the woman, her husband, and assorted neighbors and animals. As he ran, the gingerbread man taunted them with the words:

> Run, run, as fast you can.
> You can't catch me; I'm the gingerbread man,
> I ran from the little old woman and the little old man,
> And I can run from you too, I can, I can.

Who knew? Maybe I was the Gingerbread Girl. I had run away from the beer-smelling man in the movie theatre; and now from the Greek War Relief Man.

My mother was surprised to see me home earlier than usual, so I told her the story. "I hope I did the right thing," I finished. "I mean, I don't even know what a bugger *is*."

"Well *I* do," my mother said. "And you did."

*

A few days later, as we were riding on the 9:20 Sunday morning train to Ste. Eustache, Wooly asked no one in particular, "What the heck does 'plage' mean anyway?"

Plage Burnet was our destination.

"It means beach," Cath hissed. "For God's sake, don't show your ignorance." Cath, whose cousin Myrna was married to a French

Canadian, had more French words at her command than the rest of us did, but that didn't excuse Wooly's question.

"Well I didn't know for sure," Wooly airily forgave herself. "I figured it was something like that."

Cath rolled her eyes ceilingward, but Wooly just brushed her long mane of chestnut hair out of her eyes and gazed out at the unfolding countryside, oblivious. "Oblivious de Havilland," as she might have said.

Such preparations that had gone into this trip. The buying of bathing suits; the shaving of legs and underarms; the stocking up on sun tan oil; the making of picnic lunches; the going over of arrangements to meet at church at 7:00 a.m. for Mass, then get down to the station by departure time. All of these logisitics had been accomplished, and now there was just the train ride to get through.

"Do you think we'll meet any cute French boys?" Mitt asked.

"Not if they hear Wooly asking dumb questions like that," Cath said.

She was wrong. Wooly was the reason we met them. After we had spread out our towels and applied our suntan oil, a quartette of boys came along and spread out their towels a short distance from ours. They talked among themselves in French and pretty soon two words emerged from their conversation: Rita Hayworth. They were looking over at Wooly and repeating the star's name. By the summer of 1943, it was vieux chapeau for Wooly to have her looks compared to Rita Hayworth's. It was just coincidence that Wooly happened to wear her hair in the same style as Rita wore hers. Or so she claimed.

There is always one brave boy in such a group, and he stood up and walked over to our towel village to ask Wooly, "Avez-vous une allumette?"

Wooly turned to Cath with a puzzled, puckered frown.

"He wants a match."

Wooly smiled her slow Rita Hayworth smile from behind her curtain of Rita Hayworth hair, and said, "Non, je regrette."

That was okay, because he didn't want a match anyway.

"Quel est votre nom?"

Wooly understood that one. "Wooly," she said.

"Wooly?" he repeated. "C'est comique. Mon nom est Jean-Paul." He turned toward Mitt, "Et vous? Votre nom?"

"Mitt."

"*Mitt*? Wooly et Mitt? C'est très comique." He held up his hands and said carefully, "I wear wooly mitts."

We laughed.

One by one his friends drifted over. Jean-Paul indicated the other boys and said, "Je vous présent Jean-Claude, Georges, Etienne."

Wooly languidly included us in her armsweep, "Mary, Cath, Mitt."

They brought their towels closer to ours and we swam, ate, and talked together as best we could. The boy I talked with most was the one named Georges. Our conversation was largely composed of such phrases as:

"Parlez-vous anglais?"

And, "Je ne comprends pas" — said in our best French accent. So good, in fact, that they thought we were just being modest, and spoke all the more quickly, requiring us to say, "Parle lentement, s'il vous plaît." And we would say that so authentically that it would spur them on to even more animated conversation. Finally, exhausted from the effort of trying to keep up, we would say, again, perfectly, "Je ne parle pas très bien français."

It was unfortunate that most of the French lessons we had had at school had consisted in teaching us as many ways as possible of saying, and in the best possible accent, that we couldn't speak French.

The phrases got us through the afternoon until we had reason to cast anxious glances at the darkening sky. Suddenly a zed of lightening flashed, followed by a grumble of thunder, and then a cloudburst that immediately soaked everything we had with us.

"Let's get out of here," Cath shouted. We jumped up, shook the sand out of our beach towels, and stuffed them into our beach bags. Then we pulled on our wet slacks and wet tops over our wet bathing suits; stuck our feet into our wet sandals, and started running.

"Hey, hey, Rita Hayworth," Jean-Paul shouted after Wooly. "Arrêtez-vous!"

"I'm getting soaked!" she called over her shoulder. "Goodbye."

"Eh, Marie! Attends-moi!" Georges yelled after me.

"Goodbye, goodbye," I sang. "Nice meeting you." The Gingerbread Girl strikes again.

Sitting on the train in our wet clothing, we looked like drowned rats. Even Rita. I mean Wooly.

Canadian Army Sails To War

Biggest Battle Yet, Declares Eyewitness

Tremendous Salvos Reach 10 Miles Inland

By Richard D. McMillan

U.S. AIRDROME, Tunisia, July 10—(B. U. P.)—A young American reconnaissance pilot told today how Allied warships dashed close to the shore of Sicily, fired tremendous salvos into the Axis defences and started "a chain of smoke and flames" stretching 10 miles inland.

"Someone is definitely catching Hell," he remarked as he brought back first pictures of fighting on the Sicilian beaches stormed by Allied forces.

Montrealers Go to Africa

Canadians Interviewed On Sailing for Africa

By Ross Munro

SOMEWHERE IN ENGLAND, (Delayed) — (C.P.)—Lord Tweedsmuir, son of the late Canadian Governor-General, joined his regiment shortly before the Canadians were due to sail for Africa . . .

There were some Canadians with the flotillas of Royal Navy assault landing craft. Aboard one ship were Lieut. Rodger Parker of Toronto and Sub-Lt. Andrew Clark of Hamilton, Ont. The latter was at Oran during the original North African landings last autumn, taking American shock troops into the beaches . . .

At one headquarters Capt. C. F. Richardson of Montreal and Toronto was serving as camp commandant. He was a song writer who before leaving London wrote a song entitled "I Think of You...

Munro Describes Embarkation Of Forces Sicily-Bound

Ross Munro, Canadian Press war correspondent who sailed with the Canadian force from Britain, left this story with Canadian military authorities telling of the departure of the Dominion force which today invaded Sicily.

By Ross Munro

SOMEWHERE IN ENGLAND— (C.P. Cable)—Secretly, quietly and in orderly fashion, this gigantic, combined operations force — they told us it was against "X" — was mustered aboard a multitude of ships in great invasion armadas at anchor in a number of British ports.

Thousands and thousands of Canadian and British troops rolled to the docksides in troop trains that came from all over the United Kingdom. There were Canadians from Southern England and others from a dozen camps in other parts of the island where they had been doing special training.

There were Scots from the Highlands and Lowlands, English and Welsh units.

We saw assault infantry come aboard their ships, loaded down with small arms and other weapons and looking husky and fit. There was an immense amount of special equipment and there were many diverse units on the beach at the base: special artillery units, airfield construction units, mine-clearing sappers, road construction units.

There were also signals and supply and ordinance services and all the panoply of an expeditionary force of major importance.

Grand Spectacle

I was at the port where there was the largest concentration of shipping and it was a grand spectacle to stand on the top deck of our infantry-landing ship and look over a harbor thick with vessels.

The invasion force was gathered amid the most confusing and wildest rumors about future operations ever heard in Britain since the start of war. Talk which went the rounds about a possible German invasion of Britain in 1940 was nothing compared to what could be heard this time in London and in towns and ports of England and Scotland.

Beginning of End for Hitler

WASHINGTON, July 10—(A.P.) —President Roosevelt considers the Allied invasion of Sicily as virtually "The beginning of the end" of Hitler's Europe, the White House said today.

Churchill Sees "Watch on Rhine"

LONDON, July 10 — (B.U.P.) — Premier Churchill went to the Aldwych theatre last night with his wife and daughter Mary, well knowing that the Allied troops were about to invade Sicily.

The show they saw was "Watch on the Rhine."

Dunkirk Hero Dies in Germany

LONDON, July 10 — (C. P.) — Brig. Claude Nicholson, the man who detained the Germans long enough at Calais in 1940 to permit the British evacuation of Dunkirk, died in a German prison camp in June, it was learned yesterday.

Brig. Nicholson was in command of 3,000 British and 800 French troops who defended Calais for five days against four divisions of Nazi troops attempting to drive through to Dunkirk. Only 47 of the 3,800 men escaped.

The town was blasted into flames by waves of German dive bombers and heavy guns when, under a flag of truce, the German command demanded that Nicholson surrender. He refused and the Germans gradually moved in. Nicholson managed to smuggle out 47 of the defenders in a British patrol boat for England before Nazi forces cleaned out his garrison.

Barometer Rising, by Hugh Mac-Lennan—A story of Canada in war time and of the great explosion which all but destroyed Halifax. A novel that is as satisfying as it is exciting and timely. **2.50**

Klee Wyck, by Emily Carr—A series of sketches of West Coast Indians written while Miss Carr was living with them. Stories written with beauty, pathos, and a sense of comedy. Illustrated with reproductions from the paintings of the author. **2.50**

Berlin Diary, by William Shirer. Here is the private personal, utterly revealing journal of a great foreign correspondent in which he tells of the things he saw during the seven terrible years of Hitler's rise to power. **3.75**

CHAPTER SIXTEEN

ORDEAL

By an incredible stroke of luck, Bob, who had just been transferred to Toronto on July 8th, was given a twelve day leave on July 27th.

When this news came, I was thrilled. After reading his letter, I went running into the kitchen, shouting, "Bob's coming home! He's coming home!" stopping just short of jumping up and down in my excitement. My mother said something like, "That's nice, dear," in a distracted way, and I felt an immediate pang of remorse for being happy when she was so worried because my father's condition was much worse.

I scarcely knew how to feel. I felt guilty about being happy. I had a foreboding that my father was going to die. I felt sad about that, but at the same time, I thought that if he did die, my mother would be spared the unrelieved torment she'd been put through all these months.

She, though never having being trained to be one, was his nurse, with all that that term implies. She brought him the bed pan, emptied it; bathed him, shaved him, changed his sheets; washed and wrung them by hand; (we had no washing-machine) and hung them out on the clothesline to dry. She cooked special dishes to tempt his appetite as she watched him waste away from the proportions of a big man to less than a hundred pounds. She had done all of these things day after day, month after month. They had twin beds, and she slept in the bed beside his, so she was never relieved from the ordeal. A registered nurse would have been able to leave the job after eight hours, but she was on twenty-four hour duty.

Because of the medication he took, and the pain he was in, he didn't even realize all that she was doing for him. One day, however, after she had wiped his forehead with a cool cloth and given him his 222's, he said to her, "You are my sunshine." That was the name of a song that had been popular a couple of years before. His saying that set her up for days.

After attending to his needs, she would go out to the kitchen, the room that was her true domain, make herself a cup of tea, and sit down at the kitchen table to drink it, and perhaps catch up with her reading. Or she would pick up her rosary, which was always lying on the kitchen buffet, and say a decade or two.

After Cath and I saw a production of "Our Town" where the girl in it, Emily, realized after her own death that she had never really looked at her mother's face, I made a point of looking directly at my mother more often, and studying her.

She had been in her early forties when I was born, but there were no lines or wrinkles on her face, even after all those months of looking after my father. Her skin was soft and smooth, her cheeks and chin, firm, and plump. Only her neck betrayed signs of aging. Incredible as it may seem, she was always cheerful and good-natured. Her even temper wasn't faked; it was her natural disposition. Perhaps its was a familial trait. When her father's cousin, Joseph H. Choate, a lawyer and U.S. Ambassador to Britain, was in his 80s, he wrote in his autobiography, "I have never had my horoscope cast, but it must have been propitious to account for the cheerful temperament which has marked my whole life, always looking on the bright side and making the best of everything as it came." My mother could have described herself in the same fashion. All her life she bore a strong family resemblance to Joseph Choate, so it may not be coincidence that their dispositions were similar.

But over the six months of my father's illness I noticed the look on her face changing. When she was unaware of being observed, her expression was one of infinite sadness.

On the third day of Bob's leave, which was my last day of school until the fall, he came to pick me up and drive me home. When we turned down my street from Sherbrooke, we saw an ambulance from St. Mary's Hospital parked in front of the flat. My stomach lurched when I saw it. The ambulance attendants were just sliding my father's stretcher into it.

112

My mother got into the back of the ambulance with him, and we told her we'd drive up to the hospital to get her and bring her home.

Bob came over the next day, and just as I let him in the front door, the phone rang. It was the hospital calling my mother. We could tell it was an important message, so we went into the dining-room to stand beside her. When she hung up, she told us, "That was the doctor. He says that Dad has cancer of the colon. And he has only a few days to live." Then she broke down. I put my arms around her and started to cry too, then Bob put his arms around the two of us, doing his best to give us comfort.

"Can I do anything to help?" he asked, after we had pulled ourselves together.

"Yes, the first thing is to send a telegram to Choate in Halifax," my mother said, "I'll phone the rest of the family."

So Bob and I went to the telegraph office, then he drove us all to the hospital and waited downstairs while we went in to see my father, who didn't recognize any of us.

Bob spent his leave on call, ready to drive us back and forth to the hospital at any hour of the day or night, and on the ninth day of Bob's twelve day leave, my father died.

*

I had thought, while my father was sick, what a shame it was that he was too sick to feel like reading. He had been such an avid reader all his life, and for the last six months of it, while he was in such pain, it might have helped to take his mind off it.

While the fathers of some of my friends drank to escape the grim quotidian, my father read. But I noticed some parallels between my friends' fathers addiction to alcohol, and my father's addiction to books. Just as their fathers devoted much time, effort, and money to making sure they had something to drink, so too did my father ensure that he always had something to read.

"When I get a little money, I buy books," Erasmus, the Dutch scholar wrote to his friend, "and if any is left, I buy food and clothes." The first time I heard my father quote that was during the Depression, when he sheepishly explained to my mother why he hadn't bought the new fedora he badly needed, because of the book he'd bought instead.

And while it's true that I never had to stand outside a library calling, "Father, dear father, come home with me now," his reading habit affected me in other ways. One evening while I was still in grade school, when I went to pick up some books for him at the lending library, Mrs. Wand was busy with other book-borrowers, and I had an extended wait. As a result, I didn't have time to finish my homework. The next day, when the teacher asked why it wasn't done, I explained that I had gone to the library for my father, and had to wait a long time.

"Do you mean to tell me that your father sent you to the library, instead of overseeing your homework?" she asked scandalized.

"Overseeing" my homework. That would be the day. I don't think he even knew I had homework. When I mumbled, "Yes," she sniffed, "Your father isn't very conscientious." I was mortified at having her say such a thing about him in front of the whole class, and I could feel everyone in the classroom looking at me. Imagine having a father, they must have been thinking, who isn't conscientious (though, like me, they probably didn't know what the word meant).

The teacher's words came back to me after he died. It was probably true that he hadn't been very conscientious about fatherhood — at least since I was born. Perhaps he did spend too many hours in that chair, reading. Maybe it was because I came along when he was fifty, and he thought the fathering phase of his life was behind him.

But possibly if that teacher had known of his legacy to me she wouldn't have judged him so harshly. Because, over the years, all that talk of his about books; all those apt quotations; all those casual references to writers, living and dead; and all those trips of mine to McArdles Book Store and Wand's Lending Library must have had a subliminal effect on me. For without being aware of it, I was developing what was to be a lifelong love of the printed word.

Readers Today Show Preference For Stories Without a Problem

Romance is in the air this spring. This can be seen not only in the large number of girls appearing veiled at the altar but also in such things as reading tastes. The Y.W.C.A. Library confessed Saturday to a growing demand for romances for spring and summer reading.

One caller went so far as to ask for "a love story with a sad ending." The librarian believes that people surrounded on all sides by war and its difficulties ask only to he entertained when they pick up a book. As one reader put it: "I want to read something that will help to get the war out of my hair for an hour or two." Not only romances are enjoying unprecedented popularity but also good stories "without a problem." In other words it seems that people are meeting enough problems in real life and can do without them nicely when they read, said the librarian.

Armchair travellers do not roam as much in summer. "Better Golf Without Practice" and "Budget on Tennis" are replacing "Land Below the Wind" or "The Donkey Inside." One man admitted to the librarian that he always read tales of polar life and exploration in the hottest weather, finding that holding the thought of snow and icebergs helps greatly to counteract both heat and humidity. Another reader finds the best antidote for hot weather a blood-curdling mystery, when any perspiration bedewing the brow can be laid to fright and not to the mercury.

Both men and women patronize the Y.W.C.A. library and books are carefully selected to suit all tastes. There is a well-supervised selection of children's books.

Summer hours begin tomorrow and last until September 2. They are: Monday, Wednesday and Thursday, 12.30 p.m. to 6 p.m.; Tuesday and Friday, 10 a.m. to 12 noon, 1.30 p.m. to 6 p.m. Saturday, 10 a.m. to 1 p.m.

Courtesy of *The Gazette*, Montreal

Montreal Star Aug. 27, 1941

Editor Calls Silence Crime

R. S. Kennedy, Montreal, Urges Use Of "Great Language"

VICTORIA, Aug. 27—(C.P.)— Use of more "great language" by Canada's leaders during the war was urged yesterday by Roderick S. Kennedy, Editor of the Family Herald and Weekly Star of Montreal, in an address to the Canadian Authors Association convention here.

"There has been a crime committed every day since the war began in Canada in connection with the war effort — the crime of silence on the part of those who are our war leaders, and I do not speak of any particular party or creed," Mr. Kennedy declared.

"Not all of us have the fibre to do all we can in this war unless we have a little spark of inspiration to get us going," he said. "The lack of such inspiration is resulting in a coolness which will prevent us from making a full material effort."

The forces arrayed against the British Commonwealth were too efficient and too mighty to permit of anything but the greatest effort, Mr. Kennedy said.

"We see those around us failing to make such an effort," he declared, "and it is my claim that one of the chief reasons is the lack of great language spoken in a great way at the right time."

Montreal Star Aug. 31

Good Reading Personality Aid

THERE is as much need to renew your mind as there is to renew your wardrobe, hairstyle and house furnishings. Outmoded ideas, patterns of thought and vocabulary will date a woman just as quickly— if not more quickly— than past-vintage clothes and a bun on top of her head.

Best way to equip your mind with new mental furnishings is to read. Keep abreast of what's happening in the world today. Using your newspaper as a guide, follow through on topics in books on history, foreign policy, personalities in the news, air power or geopolitics that will give you a comprehensive knowledge of special subjects.

While you're reading, gather together a new vocabulary. And while you're at it, retire any threadbare slang that dates your speech. Friends have been known to stay from a favorite tea table, because the hostess' collection of slang phrases dulled her conversation.

Montreal Gazette May 27, 1941

"Read the Newspapers"

Teacher Says That's The Way to Find Out What's Going on

PHILADELPHIA, March 28—(A. P.)—Miss Gladys Ide, Philadelphia director of special education, says school teachers "offer school children insipid stuff." "Read the newspapers and find out what's going on in the world," she told a special education panel of the 28th annual schoolmen's week last night.

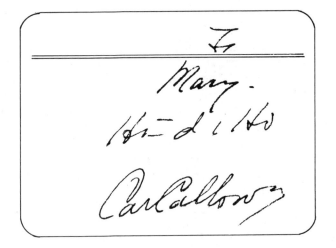

CHAPTER SEVENTEEN

WORDS

One cold end of November day in 1943, instead of taking the streetcar straight home from school, I went to Lindsay's Record Store on Ste. Catherine Street to meet Cab Calloway. He and his Cotton Club Orchestra were playing that night at Chez Maurice Danceland, and he was in the record shop to promote his records and the dance.

He published a "Hepster's Dictionary" each year and was an expert on jive talk. In fact, he was responsible for much of the jive then current, and for years had conveyed the message that the language learned at your mother's knee and other joints is an on-going, ever-changing, prismatic, and humourous thing.

There weren't many people in the store, so I had the chance to quiz him at length, and he graciously gave me the impression that there was nothing he'd rather do than discuss jive with me. I regarded jive talk a bit as I did Latin, and was interested in finding out the origins of certain words and expressions.

He told me, for instance, that in the expression, "Greetings, Gate", made popular by comedian-musician Jerry Colonna, the Gate stood for Gatemouth, not alligator, as I had thought. Gatemouth was the name given to trumpet players; the same kind of name as Satchelmouth, which is what Louis Armstrong was called, before it was contracted to Satchmo.

Also, Calloway said the word "jive" itself meant to hand someone a line, as well as being "Harlem talk". "Apple" meant the big city, Harlem or New York. "Cooling it" meant that a cat was between gigs.

"That's what my mother said when my father's friend was out of work," I told him, "that he was 'cooling his heels'."

"Your mama's hip," he said, and I laughed. "Hip", interchangeable with "hep" meant "with it", knowledgeable, sohpisticated. I thought my mother was anything but.

"That's another thing," I said. "Sometimes people say 'hip' and other times they say 'hep'. Which is it?"

"Some years it's more hip to say hep, and other years it's more hep to say hip. Dig?"

"Dig," I said.

Dig was a good all-purpose word. It meant to like, as in "I dig Sinatra." It meant to understand , as in "I don't dig algebra." It meant to meet, as in "Plant you now, dig you later." It meant to look at, as in "Dig the zoot suit with the reet pleat." And it meant to listen to or hear, as in, "Pipedown, I want to dig the music."

There was a folder advertising current records on the countertop, and I asked him to sign it for me. He wrote, "To Mary, Hi-di-hi, Cab Calloway".

Hi-di-hi-di-ho was his trademark phrase, and I asked him how come.

He said it happened one time when he was singing "Minnie The Moocher" on the radio, and clean forgot the words. Can you dig it?" he said, still amazed, "And I was the one who wrote the thing! So I started improvising with 'hi-di-hi-di-ho', and all the cats joined in, singing it back to me. The folks dug it, so I kept it in my act."

A writer named George Frazier had written an article in LIFE Magazine the month before about then-current slang, and we talked about it. Frazier had written about a form of dialogue called stichomythy — short, quick sentences. Current examples of stichomythy used by teenagers at the time were: "Whatcha know, Joe?"; "What's buzzin' Cousin?"; "What's cookin', Good-lookin'?"; "What's your story, Morning-glory?"; and "What's the good word, Mr. Bluebird?".

Frazier also had described another speech pattern called tautology — the use of the same word or similar words over and over again. I had seen an example of that in one of Bob's Westmount High School year books. A note of almost tautological hysteria was reflected in some of the favorite expressions of the 1942 graduating class:

"Oh my shattered nerves!"

"It's hysterical!"

"Mur-der!"

"Yikes!"

"Yeah Man!"

"Solid, boy!"

"Zhavves!"

"You drip!"

"It's soooooooooo gorgeous!"

"Are you suckin' for a fat eye?"

"Oh, da babe!"

"Oh, Gad!"

"Oh, solid, Jack!"

"Snark, snark!"

"Ye jerk."

"Oh lush!"

and "Seulement de bessss!"

There was also a jargon that originated in the military and was taken up by civilians:

"Snafu" — an acronym for Situation Normal, All Fouled Up (laundered version)

"Gremlin" — a gnomelike jinx that was blamed for everything that went wrong

"D.P." — Displaced Person

"Zombie" — Man on Reserve instead of Active Service

"Kopasetic" — fine, okay, on the beam

"Brassed off" — annoyed

"Nervous in the service"

"There's a war on, moron"

"As subtle as a sailor on a seven hour pass"

"That's a military secret"

"Things Are Tough All Over"

"The gen" — information

But though words and expressions were contributed to the language by servicemen, it was musicians who were most responsible for enriching our vocabulary.

In addition to Calloway, other musicians made contributions, including Duke Ellington, who seemed to have invented a whole new lan-

119

guage; Slim Gaillard, (who was responsible for the suffix "aroonie" on certain words); and Fats Waller, (whose intonation, "One never knows, do one?" was appropriated by all).

But the musician with the richest and most colorful manner of speaking was Louis Armstrong. He was a true original with a unique way of thinking and expressing his thoughts.

When describing fellow musician Bunk Johnson, who drank himself to death, Armstrong said, "He goofed his break." In a letter to the editor of the *Esquire Jazz Year Book* when telling about his and Billie Holiday's roles as lovers in the movie, "New Orleans", he wrote, "It looks so real, the folks out here really think that Billie and I are canoeing in real life." He signed off the letter, "Red Beans and Ricely Yours", similar to Mr. Pickwick, who ended his, "Chops and Tomata (sic) Sauce". And Armstrong was the one who, when asked, "What is jazz?" replied, "If you've got to ask, you'll never get to know."

He was responsible for another type of "language" as well — scat singing. Similar to Cab Calloway's experience, once he dropped his music sheet and didn't know the words, so he went on "singing" to the music with made-up word sounds similar to what he might have played on his horn. The audience so enjoyed the results, that that form of vocalizing became a permanent part of his repertoire, and was copied by other jazz singers from then on.

Other words in our vocabulary that originated in the music world were: (appreciatively) au reet, out of this world, groovy, dreamy, in the groove, solid as a stone wall, Jackson; solid sender (musician); jumpin' (band); and slick-chick — a girl who inspired a boy to make a "click-click" sound involving tongue, teeth, and cheek, reinforced with the phrase, "Hubba-hubba!"

Then there were superlatives like, "The greatest thing since canned peas," and "The greatest thing since metal-tipped shoelaces."

Pejorative expressions were: strictly from hunger; it hangs me up; brings me down; is square, nowhere, a drag, ickie, corny, schmaltzy, cornball, rugged, and grim.

Some definitions that found their way into our consciousness, if not our everyday vocabulary were:

Ickie: a square from Delaware with long hair down to there

Hepcat: root, zoot, and cute to boot

Foof: a goof sitting on a roof, acting aloof when you want to hoof

The first time I encountered the word "jerk" applied as an insult was in the 1941 movie with Gary Cooper and Barbara Stanwyck, called

"Ball of Fire" — an updated version of "Snow White And The Seven Dwarfs". Stanwyck played a singer named Sugarpuss O'Shea, who describes the Cooper character, a shy professor who was writing a piece on slang for an encyclopedia, this way: "He can get drunk on buttermilk, blushes up to his ears, and doesn't even know how to kiss, the jerk." RKO based its entire ad campaign on that description.

When I dated Tommy, who went to Catholic High, he told me that his school principal forbade them to say "jerk" because it had a sinful connotation.

When I was leaving Lindsay's Record Store, Cab Calloway shook hands with me and said, "So long, kid." I had been thrilled at being able to talk with a master, and left with some new words to pass along to Cath, Mitt, and Wooly.

My parents had a saying with regard to building a vocabulary: "Three times and it's yours." It meant that if you came across an unfamiliar word, looked up its definition, then used it appropriately three times either in writing or conversation, the word then became "yours" — a permanent part of your repertoire.

Maybe the reason we kids kept refurbishing our vocabulary with fresh words and phrases was to set ourselves apart from parents and teachers, just as the slaves on Southern plantations talked jive when they didn't want their owners to understand what they were saying. But apart from the words I'd learned that afternoon from Calloway, it was safe to assume that by the time jive words and expressions filtered down to four white teenage girls in Montreal, they were no longer au courant in Harlem.

*

Though I knew that Cab Calloway was the originator of the zoot suit — I had seen pictures of him wearing them while doing revues at the Cotton Club — because of all the trouble they were causing, I hadn't brought the subject up. The main elements of the costume were the baggy high waisted pants with narrow "pegged" cuffs, and fingertip jacket with exaggeratedly wide padded shoulders and lapels. Accessories were wide brimmed pork pie hats, long keychains that extended from belt to ankle, and a big floppy bow tie.

Someone wrote a song about the suits with their "drape shape" and "reet pleat" and the fashion probably would have died a natural death had the War Production Board in the U.S. not declared that, because of its wasteful use of material, the zoot suit was interfering with the war ef-

121

fort. This made the wearing of a zoot suit a cause célèbre. The WPB edict was then termed "persecution of a minority". The minority referred to could have been teenagers in general; Negro teenagers in Harlem, Detroit, and Philadelphia, where zoot suits were popular; or Mexican-American teenagers in East Los Angeles, where they were also a favored costume.

The fad was light-hearted until June of 1943, when rioting broke out between U.S. soldiers, sailors, and Mexican-American youths dressed in the outfits.

One of the tactics used by the sailors against the zoot suiters, was disrobing and beating them, or "pantsing" them, that is, tearing off their pants. Pictures in LIFE showed depantsed zoot suiters who had been rounded up by police, chained together awaiting a court hearing.

Eleanor Roosevelt called a press conference and blamed the zoot suit problem on the growth of racism all over the world.

In Montreal, after zoot suiters broke up a street dance in Rosemount, the Canadian Legion asked the Montreal police department, in conjunction with the RCMP, to round them up. "We always get our zoot" could have been the RCMP's new slogan.

Montreal City Councillor Frank Hanley petitioned Ottawa to stiffen clothes rationing regulations with the view to outlawing the wearing of zoot suits. The making of zoot suits was already outlawed. Tailors across Canada were required to pay stiff fines or risk a jail sentence for being caught making them.

So in addition to the many theatres of war in Europe and the Pacific to keep track of, there was this new one that had opened up on the home front.

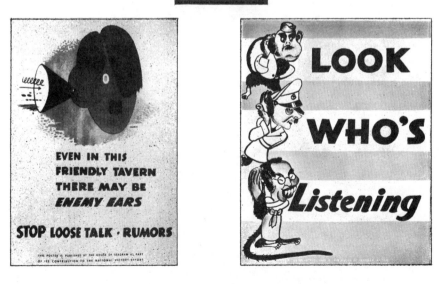

Posters distributed by Seagram–Distillers, drawn by Seymour Goff.

Loose Talk can cost Lives!

"Convoy sighted...our agents in Canada were right!"

Keep it under your
STETSON

Stetson Hats for men $6.50 up

Brock $6

Kensington $5

Women of today wear Stetson Hats too

MADE IN CANADA

JOHN B. STETSON COMPANY (CANADA) LIMITED

Legend of the "Gremlins"

PILOT OFFICER Cyril Spencer of Peterborough, crew leader of a Halifax bomber, who is now a prisoner of war in Germany, has been revealed as the discoverer of the "Gremlins"—the small gnome-like jinxes which are said to fly along with all R.A.F. crews.

Spencer's bomber originally was known as "G for George." Spencer disliked the name and changed it to "G for Gremlin." He drew a funny, mischievous-looking gnome on the cockpit to represent the "Gremlin."

Before taking off for raid on Germany, each member of the Halifax crew solemnly saluted the "Gremlin" mascot, asking it for "safe passage."

Often when diving through the anti-aircraft barrage over German cities, Spencer was heard shouting through the bomber's intercommunication p h o n e: "Come on, you little Gremlins, smash up this flak."

All the members of the Halifax crew swore the "Gremlin" saved their lives in many tight places.

Before the Halifax made its last flight four of the six crew members gave the Gremlin the usual salute. They were save and taken prisoner when the bomber crashed. The other two, who failed to give the salute, were killed — or so the legend goes.

Courtesy of *The Gazette*, Montreal

CHAPTER EIGHTEEN

WOMEN'S WORK

When I received my diplomas for shorthand and typing in early December, I thought I was equipped to go job hunting. When I arrived home with the certificates that day, however, my mother told me that she'd just had a call from the principal.

"He said you have an unbusinesslike appearance and manner, and that 'you walk as if you don't care whether you get there tomorrow or next week'. And he said you'd have to change your attitude if you want to get a job."

The principal had hounded me about looking like a kid since my first day there. Once, when I had my hair in pigtails, as per the fashion dictates of the college issue of *Mademoiselle* magazine, and he spotted me, he started to follow me down the hall. I tried my best to elude him, but he chased me in order to bawl me out, so I ducked into the ladies room. When I came out, he was there, lying in wait for me, to tell me that my pigtails were unbusinesslike. (Even *I* knew that, for heaven's sake).

My mother really took what he said to heart. She took me downtown and bought me a Glen plaid suit, a beige Helen Harper pullover sweater to go with it, a couple of Tooke shirts, a beret, gloves, a purse, and stockings.

When we got to the shoe department, she told the salesclerk to bring me "sensible" shoes, not loafers. All the "sensible" shoes the shoe salesman brought out made me look like an old lady, and did nothing for my legs.

The shoes she wound up buying for me were called Anatomics for Girls, whose slogan on the box promised, "Steps to good health".

"What have I gained by health?" I apostrophized, "Intolerable dullness."

"Don't you go trying to confuse me with quotations, the way your father used to do," my mother cautioned.

I was only quoting Charles Lamb's letters to Wordsworth. The woman who taught us shorthand, and whose job it was to dictate letters to us, said we might as well hear letters that were literate in school because God knows, once we got into the business world, we never would.

The new shoes made me look as if I had a severe orthopedic problem. "Maybe they'll give me a job out of pity," I muttered.

"That's enough of that."

"With a bit of luck, I'll be looking for a job during National Hire The Handicapped Week."

"I said, that will *do*."

Then she bought me a pair of Russian carriage boots to go over the sensible shoes. What a waste. I knew I'd be back in loafers as soon as I landed a job, and the boots wouldn't fit over the loafers.

My mother had arranged an appointment for an interview at the Head Office of the CNR — with the husband of a friend of hers — and I guess she didn't want to be ashamed of me.

I had studied the Help Wanted Female ads, but the jobs that interested me required experience. One was for a copywriter for a radio advertising agency. I would have liked that, but I didn't think they'd be too impressed with my previous experience as editor-in-chief of my seventh grade paper, *The Seventh Sees*, and reporter on my high school paper, *The Student Prints*. (Very big on puns, these school newspaper namers.)

The night before I was to go to see her friend's husband at the CNR, as a dress rehearsal, I put on my new job-hunting outfit so that my mother could give me a final inspection. As I paraded into the dining-room wearing my brown Glen plaid suit, white Tooke shirt, sensible shoes, and beret, my mother sat down wearily and watched me approach, pirouette, then retreat, as we'd been taught to do for a fashion show I'd been in at Eaton's.

"Very nice, dear," she said, then sighed, "*My* little girl, just sixteen years old and all dressed up to go job hunting. This has been quite a year, hasn't it?"

She referred, of course to the long illnesses and deaths of both my father and Bob's father; my brother away in the Army; and Bob in the Air Force; the war going into its fifth year, all the depressing news bulletins; the freak extremes in weather; the epidemics; and the strikes.

Back in February 1943, a cold wave had snapped all along Eastern Canada and The United States. The minus 50 degree temperatures had killed 26 in the U.S., caused frostbite, fuel shortages, schools to be closed, and work delays. In addition, it brought on an epidemic of la grippe, closing Quebec schools.

Then, at the beginning of March, there was a record snowfall that paralysed the city of Montreal and its suburbs. At the end of March, when Bob's father and my father were both in the hospital, Montreal tramways went on strike.

November brought a second epidemic of influenza, scarlet fever, in Quebec, Ontario, and Western Canada.

Now, in December of 1943, Quebec's schools were again closed, due to a flu epidemic; and Montreal was reeling from the effects of a strike by policemen, firemen, and civic employees and yet another tramway strike.

Our trials and tribulations had been almost bibical in their magnitude, and that thought must have crossed my mother's mind, prompting her to go into the living-room and return with the Bible in hand. Sitting down, she turned to the book of Job and compared calamities. After reading a while she closed the Book with a snap and said with gallows humour, "Well, at least we didn't have boils."

*

Though the skills I had acquired equipped me for an office job, I never felt that office work, teaching, and nursing were the only jobs open to women. I knew, from my father and from reading newspaper stories and magazine advertisements, that with the proper education, training, or talent, when it came to female employment, the sky was the limit.

Or rather, even the sky wasn't the limit, there being numerous accounts of women pilots in news stories and ads. Camel cigarettes ran an ad campaign featuring women in the air. They depicted women test pilots; women Civil Air Patrol pilots guarding the coast lines, and delivering war equipment; and a woman pilot who trained male pilots for the Army and Navy.

Another contributing female pilot was a nun, known as "The Flying Nun", who, in addition to flying, had developed a five tube transmitter-receiver radio set.

Women also worked as "Hangar helpers" at airports; airplane spotters in the Air Warning Service; airplane machine-gun test-firers; bomber builders, and parachute packers.

An article in *The Montreal Star* proclaimed, "WOMEN'S WORK IS WHATEVER SHE CAN DO", and cited as occupations then being held by women, that of Ice-woman,(a 90 pound woman delivering 1,500 pounds of ice per day to household ice boxes); a woman fight promotor, who not only promoted the bouts, but instructed her boxers in the manly art; and a woman railway station agent, who also acted as telegrapher and baggage master.

"EQUAL WORK FOR EQUAL PAY" was the slogan of 300 working women in England who represented 300,000 of their sister workers in every type of industry. In May of 1943, that principle was already in practice in New York State's war plants.

Women ambulance attendants on the home front replaced interns on ambulances, administered first aid, and rushed emergency cases to hospitals.

Women worked on assembly lines; in munitions plants; as punch press operators, welding torch wielders, grocery clerks, paid child care workers, and telegram deliverers.

Women also did farm work. The Land Army was divided into the Farm Girl's Brigade, and The Women's Land Brigade. They worked in farm dairies, cared for livestock, and plowed fields.

Then there was The Farmerettes Brigade, which was composed of city girls 16 and over, living in Land Service Camps in farming districts, and working 8 to 10 hours a day for 24¢ an hour.

In addition, there were the women in the three branches of the armed services; The Canadian Women's Army Corps, also known as the CWACS; Women's Royal Canadian Naval Service, a.k.a. the WRENS; and the Royal Canadian Air Force, Women's Division, a.k.a. the W.D.'s, or, less frequently, the CWAFFS.

*

There was a complicated routine that you had to go through in order to apply for a job during wartime. First you had to go to the National Selective Service office to obtain a job-seeking permit. After doing that, I went to the CNR, where I was given a test, at which I acquitted myself well enough so that my mother wouldn't have to be ashamed of me, and my mother's friend's husband phoned around to the various departments of the CNR trying to get me a place. They were all filled, so he recommended that I go to the Underwood typewriter office to be interviewed by a Mrs. Kieran, who placed people in stenographic and secretarial jobs.

The first job interview that Mrs. Kieran sent me on was to an ancient dark brick building on Victoria Square, across the square from the Canada Steamship Lines Building.

As I got off the creaky old elevator and stood outside the door bearing the company's name, I looked down at the Russian carriage boots covering my sensible shoes, and instructed them, as Mantan Moreland, the black actor did, "Feets, do your stuff". Then I straightened my shoulders and walked in.

A very pregnant woman took my name, escorted me into my prospective boss's office, and introduced us. Then she brought him a cup of tea, and he said, "Bring a cup for Miss Todd, too, please." Miss Todd! Jeepers. It must have been my businesslike outfit. Or the sensible shoes.

He interviewed me over a cup of tea, which was cozy and put me at ease, as it was cold and dark out when I got there at four o'clock. He dictated two letters, which I typed out, letter perfect, and then he told me I was hired.

The terms were: Salary, $82.00 a month; hours, 9 to 6 weekdays, and 9 to 1 on Saturdays; an hour and half for lunch; and the boss would drive me home in his car pool.

I talked it over with my mother and we decided that each month I would give her half of my pay cheque for room and board, and with the rest I'd pay for my clothes, streetcar fare, lunches, entertainment, makeup, and toilet articles.

As I prepared to plunge into the icy depths of the stenographic pool, I wondered if foreign correspondents like Johnny Jones had started this way. I knew that Chuck Dickens had.

EQUAL WORK FOR EQUAL PAY: Working high above the tracks, these women put finishing touches on the redecorating of railroad station in Kent, England. Hundreds of thousands of women like these are working at difficult but essential jobs, left vacant by men who entered the service. With "Equal pay for equal work" their slogan, 300 working women, representing 500,000 of their fellow workers in every type of industry, minced no words in stating their war and post-war demands at a meeting organized in London by the Transport and General Workers' Union. Every delegate who spoke raised her voice against sex discrimination in industry and opposed retention of women workers at lower wages than those paid to men

Courtesy of *The Gazette*, Montreal

CHAPTER NINETEEN

ALGAE IN THE STENOGRAPHIC POOL

When I arrived home after my first day at work, my mother asked, "How did it go?"

"Well for one thing," I replied, "the president of the company swore at me."

"My word," my mother said, her hand finding her throat. "Why did he do that?"

"I guess because he's nervous," I said. "He's an old man about 80, but he's chairman of about ten boards and owns all kinds of companies. He just comes in for a few hours a day. I was told all about him as I was hanging up my coat. Everybody calls him F.H., but not to his face. My desk is right outside his office, and when he walked by, I was looking at the striped morning pants he was wearing like the ones Mr. Côté, the School Inspector, used to wear. And guess what? He had a patch on the seat of them."

"For heavens sake."

"Ya, so I knew he *must* be rich."

"Don't tell me you mentioned the patch to him," my mother implored.

"Of course not. The problem was my desk. It's old, but not old like an antique, just old. In fact everything in the office is old, including the people. You should see my typewriter. It looks like the original one Mr. Underwood invented. And the phones that the men in the center of the office use — they're all on things like little expanding gates — you know, like the kind people put in doorways to keep babies in a room?"

"But why did he swear at you?"

"My desk has one of those trays in it that you pull out to put something on. And just as old F.H. came by, I was pulling the tray out, and I got distracted by seeing the patch on his pants, and I pulled the tray *right* out, by mistake. Then I dropped it on the floor, and it made a terrible racket."

"Oh dear."

"F.H. almost jumped out of his skin. He whirled around and yelled, 'Jesus Christ, girl. What the *hell* do you think you're doing?' "

"Oh, my."

"And on my first day, too."

There I'd been, trying my best to look like Kitty Foyle, the white collar girl, only to get sworn at by an octogenarian millionaire with a patch on his pants. When I dropped the tray, everyone stopped typing and working on their adding machines. The man named Cliff, who looked like Harry James, stopped talking on the phone, and hung it up on its little gate, and they all looked in my direction to see what the new girl would do next. If they were expecting anything dramatic, I disappointed them.

"What did you do?" my mother said, seeming not to want to know.

"I went to the ladies room."

I hid out in the ladies room for a decent length of time, then returned to my desk, and my boss called me in to dictate some letters.

The company I was working for were manufacturers of wire rope with the trade name TRU-LAY, so, with a burst of inspiration, since my boss ended his letters with the words, "Very truly yours", I signed off one of his letters with the words, "Very Tru-lay yours".

He made me type it over and told me to "pull up my socks".

I had lunch with the pregnant woman who brought me the tea when I was being interviewed. She was showing me the ropes (the wire ropes?) because she was leaving soon. And a good thing too. She looked as if she might have the baby by the water cooler any minute.

On the way home, I got my first taste of car-pooling.

The pool consisted of my boss, the Sales Manager, who lived in Hampstead, and whose car it was; the Secretary Treasurer, an older man, who lived in N.D.G.; a harmless little man who began every sentence with "I see by the papers"; the pregnant secretary, who huffed and puffed; and me. (F.H. lived in Westmount, and had a chauffeur to drive him, natch).

Everytime the little man brought up something he had read in the paper, my boss impatiently dismissed what he said. But the Secretary Treasurer always showed some interest. It was obvious even to me that the little man wasn't on their social or intellectual level, but I was impressed with the Secretary Treasurer's consideration of him. It's easy to be snide to your inferiors; they can't talk back, but the Secretary Treasurer's kindness won my admiration.

At one point during the drive my boss asked, "Are you satisfied with your salary, Miss Todd?" What a question. Was it some kind of test? I didn't know what to say, so to be polite, I said, "Yes." Then the Secretary Treasurer said, "Here's a tip for you, Miss Todd. Never admit to your employer to being satisfied with your salary."

Now, he tells me, and for the rest of the ride, I just looked out of the car window into the dark, snow-covered street.

They continued to talk, never knowing that as Robbie Burns put it, there was a "chiel amang them takin' notes".

Woman Makes Court History By Answering Call for Jurors

FOR the first time in the history of the local Court of King's Bench a woman responded today to the calling of prospective jurors' names by the court clerk at the opening of the February Assizes.

The generally dull procedure of choosing jurors was enlivened considerably when the woman, clutching her jury summons, walked to the front of the court to be sworn. Even Mr. Justice Wilfrid Lazure, the presiding judge, joined in the general hilarity.

Court officials conceded it was all a mistake and the feminine invader was quickly exempted. The mistake was due to a question of initials.

Most of the few exemptions allowed prospective jurymen who were questioned by Irenee Lagarde, K.C., and John Bumbray, K.C., were because of advanced age. One man summoned was 84.

Following the selecting of jurymen, the court fixed dates for several of the cases scheduled to be heard.

Montreal Star Feb. 1, 1945

Day Nursery Problems Are Discussed by Speakers

League for Women's Rights Holds Annual Meeting, Elects Officers

NINETY-EIGHT PER CENT of the working mothers in industry are holding down jobs not by choice, but because they are obliged to do so in order to maintain a decent standard of living for their children, members of the League for Women's Rights were told at the annual meeting, held in the Windsor Hotel last night.

The greatest benefits from these nurseries may not be reaped for some little while, but undoubtedly in time the training the children will receive will educate them in better eating and living habits thus safeguarding their health, and their association with other children will be an aid to character building.

Dr. Elphege Lalande, director of Wartime Day Nurseries for the province, expressed deep regret that so much adverse propaganda had been circulated with regard to day nurseries and stressed the necessity of an educational program to correct the falsehoods that had been taken as gospel truth by so many parents. He deplored the fact that the Division of Day Nurseries had encountered serious difficulties in securing voluntary workers and emphasized the need for these helpers.

"The situation may be easily explained, however," Dr. Lalande stated. "The majority of young girls hold jobs. Their work is strenuous and it is quite difficult for them to do undertake supplementary work."

CHAPTER TWENTY

HEN PARTY

In February of 1944, Bob gave me the news that he was being transferred to North Battleford, Saskatchewan.

It came as a shock, because we had been spoiled by his having being stationed at Cap de la Madeleine, a mere 80 miles from Montreal. It was more as if he had been away at college than in the service, (except that he had the thrill of flying a little plane called a Cornell during the week).

He kept his car in Trois Rivières, the nearest city to the Air Force base, and drove to Montreal on weekends. We had hardly missed a Saturday night dance at Victoria Hall.

When he left, all the songs on the Hit Parade took on new significance. Their titles succinctly summed up wartime social life: "They're Either Too Young or Too Old" so "I Don't Get Around Much Anymore" and that's why "Saturday Night Is The Loneliest Night Of The Week" and "I'm A Little On The Lonely Side" because "There's No Love, No Nothin' Until My Baby Comes Home". When "He Wears A Pair Of Silver Wings" he'll be "A Fellow On A Furlough" and I'll be "So Nice To Come Home To".

Bob's departure illuminated for me something I had been subconsciously aware of — the disappearance of boys and young men. It was as if an invisible Pied Piper had traversed the land, spiriting them away.

At the Saturday night dances at Victoria Hall, standing in front of the bandstand as we so often did, we noted the differences in the band's personnel each week.

One week a musician was sitting there in civilian clothes, the next, if he was stationed nearby, he was there in his new uniform. After a while, he'd be posted overseas, and someone new would fill his chair. In a while the replacement, too, was in uniform.

The same thing happened with the boys who came to the dances. You saw the same faces week after week, so that you felt, even if you didn't, that you knew them. Then a boy whom you'd seen in a sports jacket every week, turned up in uniform, his hair in a brushcut. Then you wouldn't see him again. That had been the case with one of Bob's friends named Ian, who joined the Navy, and the friend named Bob, who joined the Air Force.

It was the same situation at Heller's. A boy who came in regularly for years would perhaps miss a few days, then reappear dressed in Navy uniform. He would self-consciously remove his cap to reveal his white-walled head and suffer the good-natured kidding, then wouldn't come in anymore.

It was noticeable in movie theatres, streetcars, offices, stores, and on the street too — the dearth of young men.

The situation spawned a social phenomenon called the "hen party".

Cath, Mitt, and I congregated for our hen parties at Wooly's apartment. Her mother was a widow who worked in an office during the week, and often went out with her friends on Sunday afternoons.

The term "hen party" was apt for these gatherings, because we often cackled and clucked, pecked, preened, and sometimes had our feathers ruffled.

We also took advantage of these get-togethers to practice up on our smoking. It looked so simple in the movies, but mastering the technique smoothly was far from easy. We didn't inhale, unless by accident, which then sent us into coughing and choking fits. When we exhaled, or rather, blew the smoke out of our mouths, we batted it away with our hands, squinting to keep it out of our eyes, then picked the tobacco off our tongue. We liked smoking because it made you look smooth and sophisticated.

136

We had our smoking heroes. Bette Davis was our all-time favorite. She could look so ticked off when she was smoking, waving her cigarette haughtily for emphasis; stabbing the air furiously; and grinding it out in an ashtray with disdain.

Paul Henreid was the smoothest smoker. In the film, "Now Voyager", he and Betty Davis had a romantic cigarette lighting ritual. He would light two cigarettes at once, then hand one to her — a gesture as intimate as a kiss.

Then there was the type of smoker we admired, like Lauren Bacall, who inhaled the smoke down to her instep, chatted, ate a canapé, drank a Martini, then exhaled twenty minutes later. She also had a trick of placing her hand on the hand of the man who was giving her a light, ostensibly to steady his hand, but we knew better.

My brother Choate could inhale, tilt his head back, open his mouth, hold a smoldering inferno of smoke swirling in his throat, then blow it out in perfectly shaped rings. We admired, too, people who could blow smoke through their nostrils, making it look as easy as breathing.

Tough guys like Dick Powell and Humphrey Bogart always had cigarettes dangling from the side of their mouths. They could talk around them, drink around them, kiss around them, eat around them, and even fight with them still held tightly between their lips.

We weren't always comfortable on those Sunday afternoons, particularly in winter, sitting as we were with the windows wide open so that the smoke wouldn't linger in the apartment to greet Wooly's mother on her return. But we persevered, and all became proficient smokers. (In retrospect it is a pity we learned our lessons so well. One of this group was to die of lung cancer in the prime of her life.)

As we smoked, we talked. And laughed. An observer may have thought that we saw humour where none existed. That observer would not have been as easily amused as we.

Mitt told of a Scottish soldier she had gone for a walk with on Mount Royal the day before. He was a buddy of her sister's boyfriend. As she told the story, she used a Scottish burr, which she did well. She could also do all of her Irish relatives' accents, and several kinds of British besides.

" 'Ye have no idea how mizz-err-able it's been in our county since the limey lads have been stationed there', he said. So I said, 'Why?' and he said, 'They're always after our lassies,' and I said, 'Oh?' and he said, 'do you know what one of those lads did to one of our gurrrrrels?' and I said, 'What?' and he said, 'He bit her brrrrrrist!'"

We fell on the floor. Later, Mitt said she was getting ticked off with Kenny, a boy she'd been seeing. "The other night he asked me to do it," she said.

"He *did*?" That was interesting. "Yes. He said it was my patriotic duty since he was risking his life for me by joining the Navy. 'Risking his life.' He's only stationed downtown on Drummond Street for God's sake!" As her voice rose, she sounded like her Irish aunt without even trying.

"Well he *could* get hit by a streetcar on his way to Drummond Street" Wooly laughed.

Wooly had a brother who was a Captain in the Army, and she was always bragging about his military exploits above and beyond the call of duty. You'd think that she was the only one to have a brother in the service. Besides my brother Choate being in the Army, Mitt's brother was in the Navy, and her sister was in the CWACs.

That day, the proud tale Wooly told was how her brother saved his entire regiment from the heartbreak of constipation. We hooted as soon as she started, and she had to raise her voice determinedly above the sound of our raucous laughter. She told how someone apparently had reported to him that all the men were constipated. "It's not funny," she said at our braying reaction. Her brother tried to figure out what caused it. Diet? The change of water? Moving to a new base? He made an inspection tour of the latrine for a, er, first hand look. As he opened the door, he saw a row of toilets, all placed high above the floor. The feet of the sole occupant didn't reach the floor, as he sat. The Captain snapped his fingers, turned, and left, the problem solved. Back in his office, he requisitioned a carpentry detail to go to the latrine at once and build a long footrest in front of the toilets. This was done, and his men were never troubled "that way" again.

This story, while it was being told, was punctuated by our hoots of laughter and rude comments. "Well, I don't think it's so funny." Wooly protested, "Constipation is no laughing matter, you know."

That sent us off again. When we finally managed to sober up, Mitt agreed with Wooly, "You're right. Savon blue. That was a wonderful thing your brother did. He should be given a citation (puff puff) — for making the world safe for regularity."

At that, Cath choked so hard on her cigarette we thought she was a goner — a good case for eschewing tobacco.

Young Men of 18 Wanted for the

CANADIAN ARMY

*One Full Year's Training Must Take Place Before
Going on Combat Duty*

ALL Canadian men who have reached their eighteenth birthday may now enlist in the Canadian Active Army. That means from the day you pass your physical tests and sign up you will receive standard rates of soldier's pay and your dependents will receive standard separation allowances. It also means that each enlisted man will receive free dental and medical care. But, it does not mean that you will be sent on combat duty at once, for each enlisted man will receive one full year's training before taking his place in the fighting line.

FREE YEAR IN UNIVERSITY 1270 young men between the ages of 17 and 22 who have university entrance and who have successfully passed physical tests will be selected for one year's university tuition. This year will apply on their B.A. or B.Sc. on return from duty overseas. Your nearest recruiting Office will give ...rs.

Here is an opportunity for young Canadians of eighteen to receive a full year of training, a real conditioning period in which muscles will be toughened, minds made more alert. A year in which to prepare for the biggest task that has yet faced us—a job of assuring freedom for ourselves and liberating millions more. It means, too, a full year's training that will make you fit and keep you fit. Regular meals, regular hours, and regular training that will put you in the pink of condition. So, if this year you have reached your eighteenth birthday, apply to your nearest Recruiting Office.

Huge Army of Women Take Part in Invasion

Canadian Girls in Khaki, British Ats Trained for Sometime; Nurses Ready

'A GROUP from the Canadian Women's Army Corps stationed in Britain has been handpicked for duties at second front field headquarters and today are poised to take off for France as soon as the smoke of battle has cleared sufficiently to make their presence useful.

For months they have been preparing for D-Day by undergoing and completing a rugged battle school course.

The course consisted of living for days at a time under field conditions, eating, sleeping and working under canvas, and generally showing the resourcefulness and endurance they will have to exhibit when, within perhaps a matter of hours now, they find themselves in the theatre of actual fighting.

To demonstrate their "toughness," the girls recently took part in Canadian Army exercises, which demanded that they live under field conditions. At 6:30 a.m. they jumped from their beds, washed in tin basins filled with cold water, and scrambled into their field uniform —slacks, high leather boots, shirts and battle dress tunics. They lined up with the men at the cookhouse with mess tins and by eight o'clock were at their typewriters, which were located in any convenient place—in a tent with a packing case for a chair or the back of a truck equipped as an emergency office. Work ended at 6 p.m. Doreen Fitzsimmons of Montreal, is with this group.

Posted For Take-off

The British A.T.S. are taking part in the invasion, too, and it is estimated they will be the biggest army of women in history — more than 200,000. Along with the C. W. A. C., they are already posed at convenient points for the take-off.

The first of them to go ashore will be the Signals and Communications Branch of the A.T.S., then the drivers, clerks and cooks.

Their daily tasks are to clear some two million words of signals at H.Q. alone, cook some two million meals, type many millions of words, drive many thousands of miles, handle the records of millions of units of war materiel — vehicles, weapons, clothing, food, loads of ammunition, parts, army pay books, etc. They will repair all kinds of equipment from watches to motor trucks.

Their job began even before the invasion for they have been packing equipment for airborne troops, the ration packs to sustain the troops during the initial landing, blood, both liquid and plasma), and a mountain of other supplies. They are also the drivers of supplies to the ports of embarkation.

As long ago as last March the A.T.S. went off home rations and on to field rations. Under the home ration system, they were given a "messing allowance" of four cents a day which was lumped in a funds to buy such luxuries as sliced herring, anchovies, mustard and condiments used to garnish the table and supply a homey touch to the drab army fare.

The dress rehearsal for Canadian nursing sisters, who for four years and more have been coming to England, ended with the news of the invasion today.

Their place is behind the front line, in Canadian general hospitals, in casualty clearing stations, field surgeries and advanced dressing stations. They are all fully trained and equipped.

Their directing personnel has had the baptism of fire in Sicily and on the Italian front. For four years their task has mainly been to look after the injuries and ailments which come with the training of a great army. Those who went to Sicily and Italy and those in the Mediterranean theatre who have been nursing frontline casualties know what lies ahead.

Plans of the Royal Canadian Army Medical Corps in which the Canadian nursing sisters serve call for an early move into newly-taken territory. Those assigned to actual invasion duty are expert in the latest discoveries in drugs and treatments and are the most experienced in Britain. They in turn will be replaced in Britain by new establishments from Canada.

Have Eye to Safety

Lieut.-Col. Agnes Neill of Peterborough, Ont., chief matron of Canadian nurses overseas, has been non-committal about the role the women under her command will play.

"If the general hospitals and casualty-clearing stations go, the nursing sisters attached to them will go with them," she said recently. "But Canadian sisters will not be sent to Europe until a bridgehead is well established.

"Recently in Italy Canadian nurses have been attached to field dressing stations, but they will go to Europe only when there is suitable accommodation for them and when they won't be unduly exposed to danger."

Prior to invasion these Canadian girls underwent no dramatic pre-invasion training as the American nurses did.

"Physical training courses keep our girls in top physical condition," said the matron. "Our girls are in general hospitals ready to move any time anywhere without any fanfare. Our job has just been to have our nurses equipped and ready for anything."

Biggest job of the Canadian nurses will not be front-line nursing but caring for the wounded brought to Britain.

CHAPTER TWENTY-ONE

FILLING TIME

While my job took care of weekdays, with Bob away in Saskatchewan, I had to find ways of filling my spare time on weekends.

After receiving new ski equipment for Christmas, Cath and I went to Mount Royal a few times to practice before getting up the nerve to tackle the hills "up north".

After a few weeks, we decided we could meet the challenge of the Laurentian mountains, and one Sunday boarded the CPR train at Westmount Station.

It seemed, Cath complained, that just as we became old enough or eligible for something it was either cancelled, banned, or rationed.

In this instance, it was the ski train called "Le P'tit Train du Nord" that we were ready for, but in the winter of 1943, the Transport Controller had seen fit to ban the little train for skiers, perhaps believing it too frivolous at such a time. The train, with slots between its yellow wicker seats to hold the skis, and its famed good tasting coffee, was a favorite of Quebec skiers.

But the Transport Controller couldn't stop the skiers from going to the Laurentians; all he could do was make them feel less special by requiring that they board the regular trains along with the ordinary Laurentian commuters, which is what Cath and I did.

When we got to Piedmont Station, we detrained, fastened on our skis, and skied over to Ste. Sauveur, to the foot of Hill 70. Looking up, I felt a pang of apprehension. It was a lot steeper than any of the hills on Mount Royal. It had a ski-tow too, which I'd never used before, always having depended on the herringbone method of getting up hill. "Come on, " Cath said briskly, "All you have to do is watch the other skiers do it for a while before you get on yourself."

As I concentrated on keeping my skis in the tracks made by the skiers ahead of me, it was a while before I looked at the hill alongside. Omigod. I was high up. Would I be able to snowplough down? All the skiers on the hill seemed to be practiced parallel skiers. I watched for the first opportunity to get off, and managed to disengage myself from the tow while remaining in an upright position. I could see Cath continuing further up the hill, but she was a better skier than I.

The refreshment hut at the foot of the hill looked like a doll's house as I snowploughed down toward it, certain that I'd never make it without breaking a leg. But somehow I made it down with bones intact and even went back for more.

After a while, we looked around the village of Ste. Sauveur for a place to have lunch, and spotted a boarding house on the main street that looked like a Clarence Gagnon painting with the snow capping its sloping roof and the smoke tufts coming from its chimney. A sign in the window said 'Cuisine Canadienne Française'. We went in. The menu, posted on the wall, was short, but ample.

Jambon au sirop d' érable

Ragoût de boulettes

Fèves au lard

Soupe aux pois

Tourtière

Tarte au sucre

We settled for the pork and beans with sugar pie for dessert, and wondered if it was all the fresh air and exercise we had had that made everything taste so great, or did French Canadian chefs have a special way with food?

Toward the end of the afternoon we skied down the Maple Leaf Trail from Ste. Sauveur to the town of Shawbridge, and were happy to see a train waiting for us at the station like a faithful and dependable friend.

142

We removed our skis; knocked the snow off them, fastened the leather straps around them, top and bottom; bounced the poles on the ground to remove the snow from their leather spokes; and as the sun disappeared, shivered, feeling the damp cold right through our Grenfell jackets.

What a haven that train seemed, and what a relief it was, after a full day of wearing them, to be able to sit down and loosen our ski boots.

On the trainride home, everyone sang, and many guzzled Molson's or Labatt's. The songs started out tame enough, but became raunchier as the train drew closer to Montreal, and the beer bottles emptied.

We started with songs like "Alouette", "Auprès de ma Blonde", and "Bonhomme Bonhomme sais-tu jouer". It became clear that if there was one thing you could count on in an uncertain world, it was that someone in every car of the train would be able and willing to lead the crowd in "Bonhomme".

As the train chugged down from the mountains, every car rang out with the song:

"Bonhomme bonhomme sais-tu jouer," the leader sang.

"Bonhomme bonhomme sais-tu jouer," we echoed.

"Sais-tu jouer de ce violon-là"

"Sais-tu jouer de ce violon-là"

"Zing a zing de ce violon-là," he sang, and we repeated it, until he had gone through all of the instruments of the orchestra, as well as the sound they made:

"a plinkety plink de ce piano-là"

"ra-tata-tat de ce cornet-là"

"Boomedy-boom de ce tambour-là"

And at the end of each verse we shouted a resounding, "Bonhomme!"

Those who were drinking beer progressed to the dirty songs like "Roll Me Over Lay Me Down And Do It Again", "Today Is The Day We Give Babies Away", and "Roll Your Leg Over The Man In The Moon". After a while Cath and I joined in, our sensibilities not the least offended by the songs' smutty lyrics. They were just part of the train's ambience, and as indispensible to the trip as ski wax.

Dorothy Dix Says:—

Some Boy Friends Unworthy

DEAR MISS DIX: My 16-year-old daughter has a boy friend who takes possession of our home by pounding on the piano and turning on the radio to a station he likes, regardless of the likes of anyone else in the household. He criticizes her dress,

calls her dumb, tells her she doesn't have to obey me and tries to get her to skip classes as he does. He tells her he doesn't have any money to take her out, yet spends $15 on himself trying to look like a second Sinatra.

My daughter tries to laugh off his lack of manners and his laziness, but I can't see anything amusing in his rudeness. Am I not justified in asking her to find a civilized boy friend who is a gentleman? Or have all the nice, well-bred boys gone to war? Just what are the chances in life for a boy of this character or for the girl who falls in love with him?

MOTHER.

Answer:

The chances for bumptious, conceited young asses, such as the one you describe, used to be absolutely nil, for nobody would put up with their arrogance and their lack of manners. They never could keep a job or make friends. Everybody avoided them as the pests they were. They were doomed to become parasites on their parents and hangers-on of pool rooms and cadgers of drinks.

But the brightest spot in the war is that it takes these young cads and turns them into men. A drill sergeant gives them the discipline that their fond and foolish mothers didn't. They are being made to consider others instead of themselves, to do the things they don't want to do and to show respect for authority. It is working such a reformation that their own parents won't know them when they come back. If the war has robbed us of many fine young men, it is paying its debt in part by turning many worthless boys into good men.

Your daughter certainly has little pride if she puts up with the insulting treatment that this ill-bred young man offers her. But I suppose now that dates are at a premium, girls feel that they must take what they can get and not be too choosy.

The only solution that I can see of your problem is for this lad to get into the army. But his type is pretty likely to find some way to wiggle out and be a home-sitter instead of a fighter.

* * *

DEAR MISS DIX: How old should a man be before he is an old bachelor? How old should a girl be before she starts dating? How long should a girl go with a boy before permitting him to kiss her? Is a girl of 16 too young for a boy of 21?

THREE BOYS.

Answer:

Any unmarried man is a bachelor, but no one would be called an old bachelor before he was 50. A girl should be 15 or 16 before she starts dating. No definite date can be set for the first kiss, but the longer a girl puts it off, the better it is for her.

A girl of 16 is not too young to go around with a boy of 21, but she is too young to marry anybody, or have a serious love affair.

CHAPTER TWENTY-TWO

WAR MOVIE LOVERS

We had just come out of the theatre after seeing "The Fighting Sullivans", a true story about five brothers who all died when the ship they served on was sunk, and Cath said, with as much wistfulness as I had ever seen her muster, "Don't you sometimes wish you were an American?"

"What do you mean?" I asked, not wanting to commit myself until I knew what she was getting at.

"Well, like when you go to a war movie like "Bataan" or "The Fighting Sullivans" for instance, don't you feel like an American, and keep hoping they'll win?"

"Well sure, because they're our allies," Mitt said,

"No, I don't mean that. Oh, I can't explain it. I felt the same way when we saw "In Which We Serve". I kept wishing I was British. Don't tell my mother I said that; she'd kill me. And in "Casablanca", when they sang "La Marseillaise" I felt like I was French. But when you're a Canadian, you don't get a chance to feel proud, because you never see a Canadian in a war movie. Do you know what I mean?"

I finally understood what she was getting at.

For years, ever since the war had begun, we had listened to soundtracks of "La Marseillaise"; "The Star Spangled Banner"; "America"; and "God Save The King". And I had to admit that with each note, my throat constricted, and my chest expanded with patriotic pride. But because the contribution to the war effort made by the Canadian armed forces was largely ignored in war movies, we were deprived of the chance to feel proud to be Canadians.

A classic example was the Bogart film, "Sahara". It had almost every nationality represented in it. Bogart is the American commander of a tank that's struggling across the desert trying to catch up with the British Army at El Alamein. In the course of their journey they pick up British soldiers, a Free Frenchman, a Sudanese corporal with his Italian prisoner, and a captured German flyer. There's an Australian, and a South African. But no Canadian.

A great deal of Canadian chauvinistic pride went untapped during the war years. If someone in a film said he was from Montreal, or Toronto, there was cheering in the theatre and foot-stomping. Or if, in a murky London fog, a soldier admitted to being a "Canuck", you wouldn't hear the rest of the scene for the whistling.

Canada's National Film Board did make some Canadian wartime documentary films like "World In Action" and the "Canada Carries On" series. A movie with Paul Muni called "Commandos Strike At Dawn" was filmed on Vancouver Island, using Canadian soldiers, sailors, and airmen in supporting roles, but it was about the war in Norway. Vancouver Island's countryside was thought to closely resemble Norway's, even down to the fjords. The hand-to-hand fighting was all done by commando-trained Canadian soldiers, who played both British and Germans, (but not Canadians).

Parts of another movie were shot in Canada, although the whole action was supposed to have taken place here. As it was being made, it underwent a series of title changes from "The 49th Parallel" to "Five Men" then to "The Invaders". Leslie Howard, Laurence Olivier, and (Canada's own) Raymond Massey were in it. Laurence Olivier, who played the part of a French Canadian trapper was coached to speak English in a French Canadian accent.

We girls went to see "The Invaders" or "The 49th Parallel", whatever it was finally called, when it came out. It told the story of six Nazis coming ashore in Hudson Bay looking for fuel for their submarine. When a Canadian bomber destroys the sub, they're stranded. They decide to make their way down through Canada to the U.S. Their first encounter is with trapper Olivier, who manages to kill one of them before dying himself, but not before uttering the immortal line, "My fadder, he fight against you las' time. We gave you wan good lickin' den, and we do it again!"

Then a religious colony of Hutterites gives them refuge. Later, one of them is captured by the Royal Canadian Mounted Police at an Indian ceremonial meeting in Banff. Then they meet Leslie Howard camping in the Rockies. He gets another one of them. Their number keeps diminishing until there is but one Nazi left, Eric Portman, who meets up with Raymond Massey in a boxcar. And then there were none. It had excitement but it made no contribution in the sodden handkerchief department; and had no stirring Canadian national anthem. And it didn't do one thing to dispel the belief held in the U.S. and Great Britain that Canada was peopled only by French Canadian fur trappers, the RCMP, Eskimos and Indians, who cavorted on the frozen tundra and the slopes of the majestic Rockies. In short, it didn't exactly stir national pride.

There was, too, a movie called "Captains Of The Clouds", involving the RCAF, with Jimmy Cagney, Dennis Morgan, Alan Hale, George Tobias, and Brenda Marshall. Bob and I went to see it after he was in the Air Force, and all through it, Bob kept pointing out all the inaccuracies in it.

Cagney played an American who joins the RCAF, and they did play a few bars of "Oh Canada" in it a couple of times, as well as "Bless Them All", and Billy Bishop made a brief appearance. All of the RCAF guys (except for Dennis Morgan and George Tobias) had British accents, which was how Warner Bros. thought Canadians sounded. George Tobias, a Greek actor, was supposed to be a French Canadian. Surely it wouldn't have been that difficult to hire a real French Canadian to play the part.

We girls usually watched war films in silence, the only sounds from us being our ragged sobs and discreet nose-blowing.

Just as musicals had their cliché situations, so too, did war movies. As the movie began, and the story unfolded; we always knew who was going to "buy" it.

That extra nice boy who was introduced in the opening scenes was sure to be a goner by the closing ones. If the camp mascot ran up to him and he bent down to give the dog a pat, one of us would mutter, *"He's going to get it."* In fact this idea was so fixed in my mind that when I got a letter from Bob saying that the airbase dog always chose Bob's cot to sleep on and that the dog always followed him to town, my blood ran cold.

And in a war movie, if there was a boy from Brooklyn with an accent you could cut with a commando knife, and a boy called Tex who played a harmonica, it was just a matter of time when they'd get it, not if.

Noel Coward's "In Which We Serve" was one film that rendered us mute with emotion. It was such a powerful, moving, and poignant story, tracing the beginning of a British destroyer, the HMS Torrin, and the sailors who manned her, from her launching at the shipyard, to her sinking by Stuka dive bombers. Wooly was at that time corresponding with a sailor, Larry, who looked very much like the young sailor in it, played by John Mills, which made the film touch us all the more.

About six months after the U.S. entered the war, Hollywood, too, began releasing war films. Just as we watched "Mrs. Miniver" coping so courageously in her suburban London home during the blitz, and couldn't hold back the tears, we cried, too, for the American nurses at Bataan in "So Proudly We Hail", the movie that introduced Sonny Tufts to a waiting world.

We shrank back in dread during the final scene in "Cry Havoc" when the nurses emerged one by one from their dugout, with their hands on their heads, knowing they faced rape and probable death at the hands of their captors.

"Casablanca" almost undid us. We became completely caught up in the story of Rick, (Humphrey Bogart) owner of Rick's Café Americaine, and of Ilsa (Ingrid Bergman) wife of Victor Laszlo (Paul Henreid) a leader of the French Resistance.

Rick's Café was the gathering spot in Casablanca for European refugees trying to get visas for North or South America. It was the love story of Rick and Ilsa that affected us the most. That, and a stirring scene in the café: German officers in the café stand around the piano and start to sing the "Horst Wessel Song", the official song of the Nazi party, and Victor Laszlo strides over to the band and commands them to play "La Marseillaise". Then he stands at attention and loudly and proudly sings,

"Allons enfants de la Patrie,
Le jour de glorie est arrivé!"

Then the German officers sing louder and more vehemently, and, one by one, risking retribution, the refugees stand up and join Laszlo, managing to drown out, and infuriate, the Nazis.

Our one complaint with the movie was its ending, with Ingrid Bergman getting on the plane with Paul Henreid and leaving Humphrey Bogart, the love of her life, behind, with Claude Rains. We saw the movie several times, and each time I had the secret hope that *this* time Bergman would change her mind and stay with Bogart.

The movie, "Hitler's Children", based on the Gregory Ziemer book, *Education For Death*, was powerful and disturbing. It showed how German children were being brain-washed to perform any act demanded of them by the Nazis.

In the same vein, was "Tomorrow The World", about a little creep, played by Skippy Homeier, who was living in the U.S. after having been indoctrinated by the Nazis.

"Since You Went Away" was a film we could identify with, in that it was about civilian life on the home front — sort of an American version of "Mrs. Miniver". It plucked at our heart strings, especially the death of the older daughter's boyfriend, played by Robert Walker, an endearing actor who starred in another bittersweet film with Judy Garland called "The Clock". It was about a couple who meet in New York's Pennsylvania Station, while the boy, a soldier, is on a 48 hour leave. Within this period of time — a familiar one in wartime — they meet, fall in love, accidentally lose each other, find one another again, and just have time for a brief wedding ceremony before he has to return to camp. "They didn't even have a chance to do it' " Mitt mourned. (Wooly called Mitt "Lascivious de Havilland").

In a movie called "Keep Your Powder Dry", Lana Turner played a New York playgirl who never got up before noon, and only then to lunch at "21" before going tea-dancing at the Plaza, to limber up for ballroom dancing at the Waldorf. She joined the WACS to impress the bank trustees in charge of her estate so that they would turn over the fortune to her, planning to deliberately flunk out once they did, and go back to New York's café society scene. But along the way she discovered formerly unrecognized patriotic reserves within herself, and the film ends with the grand old flag snapping,as the band plays "The Stars And Stripes Forever", and Lana saluting, as someone pins a medal on her proudly stuck out chest. And whoever got to pin the medal on that proudly stuck out chest was glad that he was an American too.

Such scenes made me understand Cath's question about sometimes wishing to be an American, but we all seemed reluctant to give her a direct answer. Wooly began to quote a poem we all had to memorize in the sixth grade, Sir Walter Scott's "The Lay of the Last Minstrel".

> Breathes there the man, with soul so dead,
> Who never to himself hath said,
> 'This is my own, my native land!'

Just as Catholics we were taught never to deny our faith, we also believed it would be almost as big a sin to deny our country. For myself, I thought there wasn't any harm in admitting to a certain envy of Americans.

"Sometimes I feel jealous of Americans for being so patriotic," I said, "You know my cousin Kate who lives in Cleveland? She told me once that every morning in her school they recited the 'Pledge Of Allegiance' to the flag, holding their right hands over their hearts. Then they sang the National Anthem before saying their morning prayer. I wish Canadian kids did something like that."

Wooly dramatically continued to proclaim the poem, and Mitt and I joined in:

> If such there breathe, go, (DRAMATIC POINTING GESTURE AT CATH) mark him well;
> For him no Minstrel raptures swell;
> ...The wretch, concentred all in self,
> Living, shall forfeit fair renown,
> And, doubly dying, shall go down
> To the vile dust from whence he sprung,
> Unwept, unhonoured, and unsung.

Uttering the last words in ringing tones, we confronted Cath, who backed off.

"Well anyway," she amended, "sometimes I wish they made movies about Canadians in the war so that we could get the chance to cry for them."

We all agreed on that.

Montreal Star Nov. 24, 1943

Montreal Star Aug. 17, 1942

CHAPTER TWENTY-THREE

A LOVELY WAY TO SPEND AN EVENING

It started first as a rumour. Followed by skepticism. Then insistence. Finally the first small ad appeared. And there was no need for another. Word of mouth did the rest.

The buzz created a slight hum all over the city of Montreal. One girl in a Sloppy Joe sweater would say to another, "Have you got your ticket yet?" And the other would reply, "Are you kidding! I bought mine on the first day."

Frank Sinatra was coming to the Montreal Forum on Sunday, November 19th, 1944.

It would cap a year that had seen his star shoot into the stratosphere. Even his not being able to record with musicians had not been a handicap. While they remained on strike, he made a number of records backed up by a singing group called The Bobby Tucker Singers. Because of the absence of a big band between Sinatra and the listener, the records were intimate and affecting.

What captivated me about these records, apart from the way he seemed to glide or slide from one note to another like a trumpeter or trombonist, was his pronunciation of the words in the lyrics. I felt that he need only speak to me and I'd swoon.

Once I met a girl named Joan who came from Newark, New Jersey. Because he was from Hoboken, New Jersey, we discussed him. I told her about being sent almost as much by the way he spoke as by the way he sang, and she said, "Oh, everybody in Hoboken sounds like that."

I gasped. A whole city full of people who sound like Sinatra! I made a mental note never to go there lest I make a fool of myself every time a man should speak to me.

One day I had a terrible fright while sitting on a crowded streetcar. A man was holding up a newspaper to read, and it was folded in such a way as to reveal in the big, black, banner front page headline the letters, S — ATRA. My heart began to race with fear. Something had happened to him! And it must have been bad to warrant such a headline. Then the man refolded the paper and I could read the word SUMATRA. What a relief! But it took a while for my heartbeat to return to normal.

His movie, "Higher and Higher", came out at the beginning of 1944, and naturally, Cath, Mitt, Wooly, and I went to see it.

Boys were mean about him. In the movie, when he was singing, "This is A Lovely Way To Spend An Evening" (by Jimmy McHugh and Harold Adamson), as he sang the line, "A casual stroll in a garden/a kiss by a lazy lagoon —" some dumb boy in the audience sneered aloud, "Who wants to be kissed by a lazy lagoon?" — and shattered the romantic mood.

All through 1944, the Sinatra craze gained momentum. In October, it reached its peak. When he returned to the Paramount, teenagers started lining up at 4:30 in the afternoon of the day before the doors opened. This was when New York had a curfew too. The next day, over ten thousand young people stood in line. Another twenty thousand thronged Times Square.

The bad news for those waiting in line was that when the first show was over, only 250 came out of the theatre, which seated 3,600. Girls had taken their lunch to the theatre, and refused to leave their seats, even to go to the bathroom.

On November 19th, 1944, when Sinatra came to Montreal, before leaving home, I shaved my legs, washed my hair, and put on the powder blue cashmere sweater that Bob's mother had given me for my birthday, and a matching skirt under my camel hair coat. (Who knew? I might run into him in a hallway or someplace).

We arrived early and could hardly contain ourselves as we waited for him to appear. Finally he walked out onto the stage. A wall of sound greeted him. After acknowledging the cheers and screams, he started to sing. Or it looked like he was singing. You couldn't hear a note, for the shrieks and screams. I admit to squealing too when he first came out, but even though I stopped when he started to sing, there was no chance of hearing him. Although that part of the evening was a disappointment, we were consoled by the thought that for an hour or so, we were able to see him, breathe in the same air that he was breathing out; and share the same small part of the planet with him. But if we wanted to hear him sing, we had to listen to his records.

COMING TO THE FORUM

Sunday, Nov. 19th

FRANK

SINATRA

In Person

**With An Orchestra of 50
and His Own Special Director**

Hear ."This Love of Mine"
"Night and Day" "I'll Never
Smile Again" and Other Hit
Parade Songs

His Only Canadian

Appearance.

One Night Only.

The Voice That Thrills Millions

Seats Now On Sale At Forum Box Office.
North End $1.25, Circle $2.25, Amphitheatre $3.25,
Boxes $4.00, Orchestra $4.00, All Taxes Included.
Reservations (WIlbank 6131) must be picked up before
Saturday 6 p.m.

Bogart-Bacall Bond

New York, January 31.—(*P*)—
Film actor Humphrey Bogart said
today he had "signified my intentions" toward Lauren Bacall, his
new leading lady, although he said
he was "not exactly" engaged to
her.

The intentions, he added, were
"based on future plans." The movie
"tough guy" and his wife, blond
former Mayo Methot, recently
separated.

Miss Bacall made her first appearance on the screen with
Bogart in To Have And Have Not.

Film Star Gives Salary to Britain

HOLLYWOOD March 28 —
(A.P.)—Cary Grant, signed
by Warner Bros. studio today to
play the title role in the film
version of the stage play, "The
Man Who Came to Dinner," said
he would donate his entire salary
for the picture to Great Britain
for war relief. The salary of
his most recent film also went
to British war relief.

While neither sum was disclos-
ed, a friend said "I know that
Cary doesn't make a picture for
less than $150,000." The film
will start in a month under Edmund Goulding, British director.

Courtesy of *The Gazette*, Montreal

CHAPTER TWENTY-FOUR

MANNERS AND MORES 1944

We were having a hen party at Wooly's, eating cheese dreams, when Mitt drew a letter from her purse.

"It's from Kenny," she said.

"What did he say?"

"Remember what he said to me the night before he shipped out?" she asked.

We nodded. He had really stepped up his campaign when he was leaving HMCS Donnacona on Drummond Street for parts unknown.

"Remember I told you he said he loved me, and if I gave myself to him he'd have something to think about while he was on board ship away at sea?"

We remembered.

"And remember he said that if I *didn't* give myself to him and he was torpedoed, he would die before he'd even had a chance to live?"

"Yes."

" — and that he said if I really loved him, I'd do it. Shoot, I never even *told* him I loved him."

"Did he say anything about how good it was for the complexion?" Wooly put in, laughing.

"I think that was the only thing he left out. Anyway, I'm glad I didn't fall for any of his lines," Mitt said. "Listen to how he starts the letter: 'Dear Kiddo'."

"*Kiddo*?"

"Kiddo, yes. Isn't that romantic? But that's nothing. Listen to how he *ends* the letter — 'yours till the kitchen sinks, Kenny'."

We fell on the floor.

When we sobered up, Cath said "The main reason that *I'd* never do it before marriage, is that my mother told me she'd throw me out of the house if I ever got pregnant out of wedlock."

At Cath's words, we sat quietly contemplating the idea of poor Cath, burgeoning with child, being tossed out of her parents' home into the snow. (Of course it would be snowing).

Though Cath's mother prided herself on her religiosity, it didn't sound to me like a very "Christian" thing to do — throwing her poor daughter out into a snowbank. (The snow had been falling for some time by now).

Thank goodness my mother would never do that to me, I thought. I knew she wouldn't, because she always spoke with compassion of any girl who'd gotten "into trouble".

Somehow Cath's reason didn't seem like the best one for remaining a virgin until marriage. If you have certain convictions, fine, but if the only reason you remain pure is to avoid landing in the snow —

"Do you think she'd *really* do that?" Wooly asked.

"I *know* she would. She'd die if people knew about it."

"She'd throw her only daughter out in the sn — -out of the house, just because she cared what people would think?" I asked.

"Well, yes." Cath was looking uncertain, yet defensive of her mother's position.

"I don't think that's a good reason for doing or not doing something," I said. "I mean, if you think about it, she could be just as concerned about what people would think of her for throwing her daughter and future grandchild out in the cold."

Cath's brow furrowed.

"I was reading one of my father's books of Emerson's essays," I said, "and in the one called *Self-Reliance*, he said that what you have to do is all that should concern you, not what people think."

No one commented. Such a concept was so foreign to anything we'd ever heard at home, school, or church, that I guess no one wanted to touch it.

158

" — And that's why my mother just wants me to go out with Catholic boys," Cath went on. "She thinks 'good' Catholic boys don't do it."

"They do it," Mitt said, "but not with 'good' Catholic girls."

"How do you know?"

"I know," Mitt said sagely, "Catholic boys have two kinds of girl friends. Ones they treat with respect, and the others they see for only one reason."

"What makes you so sure?"

"I know of a Catholic boy who goes out every Friday and Saturday night with one girl, but spends every Sunday afternoon after Mass with another girl — doing it."

"How do you know?"

"I heard my brothers talking about it."

"Is the girl he sees on Sunday a Catholic?"

"Yes."

That gave us pause. We were willing to accept such stories about Protestant and Jewish girls, but Catholic?"

"I don't know any Catholic girls who go all the way, do you?" Wooly asked.

None of us did. There was a girl we all knew who lived in N.D.G. who had a "bad rep". Everyone said she did it, but she wasn't Catholic.

"As a matter of fact," Mitt went on, " A Catholic boy will go out with, or even go *steady* with, a girl he doesn't really like a lot, just so he can do it with her. But when he meets a girl he wants to *marry*, he doesn't do it with her. When he feels like it, he goes to see the girl he *used* to go out with and does it with her. And he does that up until he and the girl he *really* loves, get married."

"Why would he do that?"

"Because he wants to marry a virgin, and he wouldn't respect a girl he could do it with."

Mitt, having three brothers in our general age bracket, was someone we could trust to give us the straight goods.

"I wonder what happens to those poor used girls," I said.

"Maybe they're treated like used cars," Wooly said facetiously, "and stuck in used girl lots. I can see the sign over them now, 'Used Girls! Only used by Catholic boys after church on Sundays'."

Cath asked Mitt, "Do you think there are many Catholic boys who do that, or is it only your brothers' friends?"

"There are lots," Mitt said. "Some even go to whore houses."

"They're where my mother says the white slavers take you," Cath said.

"White slavers?"

"You don't think girls work in those places of their own accord, do you? There are these men called white slavers who pick girls up off the street, drug them, and take them to houses like that to work for them."

I *had* heard Cath's mother speak of white slavers, but hadn't known what she was talking about. Once Cath and I and Cath's mother took the streetcar downtown to an exhibition of paintings done by Cath's mother's hairdresser, and when we got off the streetcar at the corner of Bleury and Ste. Catherine, Cath's mother said, "Watch out for white slavers."

Then, as we reached the curb, the filthiest, smelliest, raggediest bum I'd ever seen said something to Cath's mother that caused her to momentarily freeze, and a look of horror to cross her face. What he'd said was so filthy and disgusting, that I was stunned that such words would come out of a person's mouth, or such a thought would cross a person's mind. I thought fleetingly that he was probably what she'd meant by the term "white slaver". Now I belatedly knew.

Mitt continued with her revelations:

"I've often heard Catholic boys at Heller's after Mass talking about being in a whore house the night before."

"That would sure come as a shock to my mother," Cath said.

Cath's mother had continued her campaign that she date Catholic boys. She was really serious about it.

One time I was down at Cath's on one of those unbelievably cold winter nights when the wind was so cold, it burned. I had managed to make my way down the street by walking backwards, with the wind searing my forehead and freezing my brain. We were huddled in the livingroom as close to the fireplace as was sensible, when Cath's mother stuck her head in the doorway, and in her high Irish voice demanded, "Why aren't you girls at the Tuesdays?" The Tuesdays! Jeepers. I'd barely made it down the street, and she expected us to go all the way downtown to St. Ann's Church.

On nine consecutive Tuesday nights you could make a novena to St. Ann, the patron saint of single girls, and pray for her intercession in helping you meet a good Catholic boy. I don't know how well St. Ann herself had done boyfriendwise, but if she made saint, it couldn't have been too impressive.

The prayer you said was:
Dear Saint Ann
get me a man
quick as you can.

(A rumor once spread through our school that one Tuesday night, a girl, after uttering that self-same prayer in St. Ann's Church, came out onto the dark street, and was raped. But then girls' schools are rife with rumor.)

It was curious that Cath's mother was so naive about Catholic boys — that is, always thinking of them as being "good" and safe for Cath to go out with. The priests at our church were under no such illusions. I noticed that whenever I went to Confession on a Saturday night. When you walked into the church, there'd be long line-ups outside the confessionals where the priests were known to be lenient with penances and/or hard of hearing. The priests who had reputations for being really tough were the ones who had the short line-ups of mostly old people, who had given up sinning. Sometimes it would happen that at the last minute, a strict priest would take over a lenient priest's confessional box, and you'd be stuck with him.

The strict priests, strangely enough, were the young ones. Some sins were still new to them, and they were still capable of being shocked. The old priests had pretty well heard everything. Sometimes their hearing wasn't very good, or they pretended that it wasn't, and they didn't ask a lot of questions. But if you were ever in line outside the confessional of a strict priest, even though you were trying *not* to hear, (even if you were *straining* not to hear) you might overhear the priest say sharply, "You did *what*?" Then, "How many times?" And then your ears would involuntarily perk up, and you'd hear, "Did you have your mouth open?" or, "Were you fully clothed at the time?" Or, "Were you sitting, or lying down?" And the penitant would be squirming, "Gee, Father, please, people can hear —" Then you'd move back quickly, stepping on the toes of the person behind you, creating a chain reaction of toe treading, and the poor penitant would emerge, red face averted, and go up quickly to kneel at the altar, staying there for *ages*, saying his or her penance.

Of late I had been observing certain contradictions concerning people's thinking with regard to questions of morality.

A girl is told it's a sin to make love before marriage.

She decides to get married, while still young.

Does she get marks for avoiding sin by getting married?

No. Everyone assumes she's pregnant.

The girl has a baby within the year.

Does she gain points because it's ten months after the wedding?

No. Her husband must be some kind of sex-crazed animal.

A girl *doesn't* have a baby within the first year of her wedding. Her husband *isn't* some sex-crazed animal, right?

Wrong. She must be practicing birth control — a mortal sin.

Okay, forget about getting married. A girl, living a long street-car ride from her office, and a member of a large family, wants to get an apartment on her own, downtown, closer to her place of business.

What does she want to do that for? She's up to some hanky-panky.

How about if she moved to another city?

Sounds all right. Although it would be more respectable if she shared the apartment with another girl.

I had noticed too that among even very religious Catholics, if their friend's son or daughter announced that he or she was going into the priesthood or convent, they would be *thrilled*. After all, the Church has to keep going, and there has to be someone to administer the sacraments to them and teach their children in parochial school. But let their *own* son or daughter announce the intention of becoming a priest or nun, and it wouldn't be "Get thee to a nunnnery, go" but more like "Hie thee to a psychiatrist, do".

Thinking about such things made me agree with Miss Mowcher, the dwarf in *David Copperfield*, who said, "What a world of gammon and spinnage it is, though ain't it!"

Dorothy Dix Says:—

Wise Girl, 17, Refuses to Marry

DEAR MISS DIX: I am a girl of 17 engaged to a boy of 18. I love him very much and hope some day to marry him, but I certainly do not intend to do so until we are out of school and he is in a position to support a family.

Last week we went out with two other couples of our own age and something was said about getting married. They all agreed to except me. I tried to talk them out of the crazy idea, but it did no good

and the two other couples got married in a little town near our home. Now they are trying to make me believe they are very happy and glad they did it, but I believe deep down inside they are sorry they didn't listen to me.

But my trouble is that since that night Bill has treated me differently. He has seemed so distant. He isn't like he used to be. Do you think I did right by not marrying him then? I did only what I thought best for both of us.

JANE

Answer:

You did exactly right, Jane. You showed yourself not only a level-headed girl, but a courageous one, and the time will come when Bill will thank you on his knees for saving him from the folly of going into a marriage for which he was not prepared.

Just at the moment his vanity may be a little hurt by your refusing to marry him when the other two girls were marrying their boy friends. He may think that it indicated that you were not as much in love with him as they were with their sweethearts. Boys of that age are very touchy, you know, and they are very anxious to be thought mature, old enough to marry, etc.

But he will get over this and respect you all the more for not being over persuaded to do what you knew to be wrong and foolish. As for your friends, by their boasting so much about how happy they are, they are singing to keeping their courage up, they are putting up a bluff, and you may be perfectly sure that they are already regretting their hasty marriage.

How are they proving their pride and joy in their marriage? Have they told their parents? And have their parents set them up in homes of their own? Or are they keeping it a secret and living in fear of their marriage being found out? Are the boys able to support their wives? Believe me, my dear, the marriages that have a chance of being successful are those which are celebrated publicly and with the consent and approval of the parents and the good wishes of the community.

* * *

DEAR DOROTHY DIX: I go around with six very nice girls with whom I want to be friends, but I seem to always be saying or doing something that gets me in wrong with them. I do not intentionally offend them. How can I keep from hurting their feelings?

JINKS.

Answer:

Some people seem to be brusk by nature and to lack a certain sense that warns them about how to keep from stepping on other people's toes. They blurt out home truths when they should keep silent. They make uncalled for criticism, and even when they try to be complimentary they offend instead of please. As, for example: Haven't you heard a woman tell a wife with a philandering husband that she saw him having dinner with a pretty girl; or that the new baby a mother is proudly showing off has the Jones' hooked nose; or ask a fat woman if she isn't putting on weight?

A good way to be sure you will always say the right thing is to mentally try your speech out on yourself. If it makes you feel good, you can pass it on.

More Women Workers in '50

U.S. Census Bureau Issues Report

WASHINGTON, April 13—(Star Special) — The war's end will not be the signal for many American working women to return to their homes, the Census Bureau said yesterday in predicting that employment of women in 1950 may be greater than in 1944.

A special study called a "post-war projection" indicated that women in the U.S. labor force in 1950 will number from 17,500,000 to 18,000,000, as compared to the 17,8000,000 average in 1944. Preference for the independence of making their own living will prevent many women from returning to a housewife's status, the Census Bureau believes. Although there was an increase of 4,500,000 women in the labor market from 1940 to 1944, only 3,000,000 women became workers because of war conditions. The other 1,500,000 would have entered the field anyway.

Of these 3,000,000 war-induced labor force entrants, 1,500,000 were girls and young women from 14 to 25 years of age. Normally about half of these, or 70,000 would be in school. The bureau pointed out, and past experience indicates that most persons who withdraw from school early to accept employment never return to school. The remaining 800,000 of this age group are mostly servicemen's wives it found, and withdrawals from jobs are likely to be particularly heavy among the wives of the returning servicemen. Many servicemen, however, will not return and many of those who return will not be able to work, the report points out. In some homes, women will have to continue to work as a replacement for these men who would have been the chief wage earners.

Eyebrow Pencil Taboo

British Women Warned Cosmetic and Gas Mask Don't Mix

LONDON May 13—(U.P.)—Don't wear eyebrow pencil in an air raid, the ministry of home security has warned women.

Eyebrow pencil of the non-waterproof type is liquefied by the temperature inside a gas mask and it runs, with dire effects on the eyes. The resulting impulse is to take off the mask, whereupon gases would take their intended toll.

C'est la Guerre

Patriotic footwear features stitched soles, pegged heels, plastic ornaments, ties instead of buckles and—no metal.

CHAPTER TWENTY-FIVE

MR. WHATCHACALLUM WHATCHA DOIN'
TONIGHT?

Christmas 1944 was a season of highs and lows.

In mid-September Bob arrived back from the Service Flying Training School in North Battleford, Saskatchewan, a full-fledged pilot, having graduated, received his wings, and been made a sergeant. He had been trained as a fighter pilot in 13 F.T.S. Course 101 which was made up of pilots from England, Australia and New Zealand as well as Canada. After a two week leave, for which I quit my job so as to be able to see him every day, he was stationed at Three Rivers, near Cap de la Madeleine, for an eight week Commando Training Course, after which he was to be shipped overseas.

After he had finished the rigorous intensive training that rendered him lean and mean, and capable of killing in hand-to-hand combat, he phoned to glumly tell me the "good" news.

"It seems that the Air Force has trained too many pilots, so we've been honorably released, and put on Reserve."

I was ecstatic. "You're kidding! That's super! You won't have to go overseas. Aren't you *glad*?"

"No, I'm not."

"You're *not*? How come?"

"Because I've spent the last year and a half learning how to fly, and training to fight, and now I find out they don't need me."

Try as I could, I found it difficult to empathize with him, so he tried to explain.

"It's like — well, I used to be on the track team in high school — and it's as if I were standing behind the starting blocks, and the starter says, 'On your marks', and I get all prepared, and then he says, 'Set', and I get all ready, and he raises his gun, and he's just about to squeeze the trigger, when he says, 'Aw the hell with it'. I feel the same kind of let-down."

From the high of Bob's news that December, we went to the low of hearing that everyone's favorite bandleader, Glenn Miller, was reported missing. On December 15th, a small plane he was in disappeared on a flight from England to Paris during bad weather. He was the Director of the United States Air Force Band, and was on his way to make advance arrangements for his band's arrival in Paris a few days later. No trace of his plane was ever found.

If somehow the Nazis had known he was on that plane and shot it down, they couldn't have struck a worse blow to our morale. Everyone was stunned by the news. People felt as if they'd lost someone close to them. Hadn't his music been the background music of their everyday lives since 1939? It was everywhere: the thrice weekly radio show for Chesterfield cigarettes; in juke-boxes, and on records at dances. They had been wooed, won, and wed to his music.

Like the musical score on a motion picture soundtrack, it always seemed to be playing in the background at important moments in our lives. You met each other with "At Last" playing in the background; you courted to "A String of Pearls"; and fell in love to "Serenade In Blue."

Just as Cath and I had cried together on the phone at the end of his last radio broadcast for Chesterfield, so too did we cry when the sad news of his being missing came through.

Another low point was that it was my brother Choate's first Christmas overseas. It would have been his second Christmas overseas had it not been for his suffering a ruptured appendix in Halifax mere hours before he was to board ship. After he recuperated, he was given embarkation leave in Montreal in August of 1944, then shipped out in September. He phoned his wife from Halifax to say goodbye, then phoned our home to say goodbye to us, but wasn't able to get through because, as my mother and sister never let me forget, I was on the phone, having one of my extended conversations.

That Christmas, what was left of our family: my mother, Helena, Bill and I, sat at the diningroom table half-heartedly eating our Christmas dinner. It was no merry Dickensian repast. Without my father, who had always done the carving, my mother had really hacked up the turkey. And without Choate there providing comic relief, the meal was a dreary affair.

Suddenly a memory came back to me, and I said, "Hey, do you remember the Christmas that Choate demonstrated those airplanes in Eaton's basement?"

My mother smiled, remembering. "Of course I do. Wasn't that fun, when he came home?"

The incident we were talking about happened during the Depression, when Choate was going to college. During the Christmas break he managed to get a job, to help out with his tuition. The job was demonstrating paper airplanes in Eaton's basement, but in Toronto, not Montreal. Why they had to import airplane demonstrators from Montreal when there must have been just as many available in Toronto, remains a mystery. Perhaps it was because he was such a whiz at flying them, and had the gift of the gab. He practiced in our basement, which had lots of pillars in it, and he could actually, by putting a little english on it, get the plane to go around the pillars and come back to him. The planes sold for 5¢ each. Once he had his flying technique perfected and his spiel down pat, he left for Toronto by train, to raise his tuition fees.

He arrived back home on Christmas morning with the most enormous box in tow. (So enormous, that he later made me a sit-in doll's house out of it).

With great ceremony, he opened the cardboard carton, and inside were what seemed to me to be dozens of presents for every member of the family. He was like a nineteen year old Santa, come by train. He handed me three boxes, which turned out to contain Tootsietoy metal doll house furniture for a living-room, kitchen, and bathroom.

"I didn't know which room you'd prefer, so I bought all three," he explained airily, at my stunned look.

The other gifts he distributed to the rest of the family were met with equal surprise at such largess.

It wasn't until all the presents had been opened and we'd finished eating our Christmas dinner, that he confessed, with some chagrin, what had happened.

167

After receiving his pay on the afternoon of Christmas Eve, he felt so full of the Christmas spirit that he went all through Eaton's like a whirlwind, buying gifts left and right, until he discovered he had just enough money left for his train fare home. When he finished his story, he spread his hands and said sheepishly, "So here I am, Mammy, right back where I started from." (He called her Mammy because Abner Yokum called his mother Mammy, and he was always quoting Li'l Abner, saying such things as, after a meal, "'Twaren't good, but 'twar fillin' "). But maybe he wasn't quite right back where he had started from. He'd had all the fun of demonstrating the planes, and of shopping, and spreading all that Christmas cheer at home.

But the best thing about it was that now, on this Christmas of 1944, years later, he had spread that Christmas cheer again. Just remembering that day had brightened us all up enough so that we enjoyed the rest of our Christmas dinner.

Who would have thought that his Christmas spirit would have glowed for such a long time? It seemed that it only had to be rekindled in memory to spread its warmth anew.

Major Glenn Miller

War Cuts Down Old Toy Supply
Of Montreal West's Santa Claus

War and its attendant difficulties has cut down the work of the Santa Claus of Montreal West. "I'll be lucky if I get 600 toys this year," declared J. J. Kirkpatrick, 41 Fenwick avenue, in a recent interview.

"The year before last I repaired some 2,000 toys; last year it was 1,600 and now I'm way down."

The 84-year-old St. Nicholas has spent almost 20 years repairing old toys for poor children so that they may find something in their stockings on Christmas morning, but this year, war has made it difficult.

"I hate to ask my friends for the use of their cars to pick the toys up. They have no gas these days. That means most of my toys now come only from around Montreal West. That's not all, lumber is expensive and its hard to get clear wood; metal is almost unobtainable, and Santa Claus has been giving clothes and useful things during the past few years so kiddies hang on to their old toys.

He only has about 150 dolls this year, girls aren't playing with dolls, he finds. They prefer soft ball and "tomboy" toys. The modern woman has even reached into the nursery!

The story of how Mr. Kirkpatrick started his odd occupation is a tale in itself. Some twenty years or so ago, he was reading a magazine a few days before Christmas. A picture caught his eye. It was of an alley in a tenement district. A little girl in one window held up a doll without any clothes—but still, a doll. Another little girl in the opposite window didn't have a toy and big tears rolled down her cheeks as she looked at her lucky neighbor. The caption for the picture was "Christmas Morning." That picture "got me," declared the white-haired Mr. Kirkpatrick. "I decided to do something about it, but you know how hard it is to start. On a trip to New York I met a lady who told me of the work American girl scouts were doing mending old toys. On my return, I got in touch with the Girl Guides here who were doing the same thing and began to work with them. Eventually, when they turned to new work, I went on on my own. The Montreal West Women's Club hooked up with me and we've being doing it ever since."

He works all year so that on the one big day poor youngsters can have a bit of fun.

Flood of Last-Minute Shopping
Tangles Traffic In Streets, Shops

Montreal's million did their last minute Christmas shopping yesterday and in the process succeeded in tying up traffic seriously and completely exhausting the city's salesclerks.

Long lines of purchasers of bottled cheer made their appearance at the doors of the liquor vendors' shops at an early hour and the lines lengthened as the day wore on.

Business in most down-town offices came to a standstill almost before it started — with the exchange of presents and good wishes becoming the important matter of the day.

Street cars were jammed and threaded their way slowly in all directions, their doors emitting crowds of holiday-makers burdened with bundles at every stop.

Taxis sought to carry only passengers who were on urgent business but even this proved more than the ration-restricted trade could handle and taxi-company switchboards began the day with replies of "not for a half hour" and after noon just threw up their hands.

Delivery boys wrestled with the myriad packages wrapped in gay paper and ribbon and dashed here and there with belated greeting cards and gift cigars, cigarettes and candy.

Uniforms of all services dotted the huge crowds that plodded their way through the streets and shouts of greetings rang out over the heads of the merrymakers and shoppers as servicemen on furlough recognized buddies.

Despite rationing, stores selling produce struggled to fill as many orders as possible, but in a great many cases found themselves unable to please everyone.

There was little grumbling, though, and good-natured banter invariably turned to mutual shoulder-shrugging as customer and salesperson alike tried to make the best of the situation.

Hotel staffs labored frantically to handle capacity houses and in addition cater to those attending the many functions held there.

Telegraph messengers, their ranks depleted by the war, rushed here and there with a grin on their faces, pocketing tips and wishing every day was Christmas.

Railway terminals bulged with incoming servicemen on leave and outgoing holiday-seekers on their way "home for Christmas."

Despite the war, the Yuletide spirit prevailed, though it must be admitted the mass looked a bit frayed at the edges.

Courtesy of *The Gazette*, Montreal

Fatally Wounded

MISSING AGAIN

KILLED

INJURED
Royal Canadian Artillery

WOUNDED

Montreal Flier
Killed in Crash

MISSING   KILLED

KILLED IN ACTION

MISSING IN AIR OPERATIONS   SERIOUSLY WOUNDED

DIED OF WOUNDS   *Official Army Casualties*

CHAPTER TWENTY-SIX

THE UNKNOWN SOLDIER

One day I was sitting on one of the long wicker benches on the streetcar, rather than in the double seats up at the front, when a woman got on, looking terribly upset. As she came down the aisle of the car, she glanced at me, and said, "Marilyn?"

I did one of those stupid things — pointed at myself and said, "Me?" — as if she could have been talking to someone outside the window behind me. "No, I'm Mary," I said, equally inanely, and she sat down heavily beside me.

Speaking with a trace of an Irish brogue, she said, "You looked like Marilyn for a second, one of my daughter's friends. I'm sorry. I'm so upset. I've just had some terrible news and I'm on my way now to — oh it's so awful, I can't believe it! I just got word that my dearest friend's son was killed in the Army!"

"Gee, that's too bad," I said inadequately.

"It's so tragic — his father was killed in the last war."

"He was? Gee, that's —"

"It's so dreadful! I was with her when she got word that her husband was killed. That was — 28 years ago. It was horrible! She was expecting this baby at the time. They were newlyweds. She was almost inconsolable. The only thing that kept her going was that she was expecting this child. That, and her religion. And now the same thing has happened! I don't know how to face her! What can I say to her? It was our priest who phoned me with the news. I haven't spoken to her yet. I just ran up the street and got on the first streetcar."

"I'm so sorry," I said.

"Her husband was a lovely boy. He went all through Loyola. A very good student in high school. Very smart in college. And a lovely person. They were just crazy about each other. Then he joined the Army. The telegram said he'd been killed in France." Her voice broke into a kind of wail and she put a handerkchief to her streaming eyes.

"The principal of Loyola wrote her such a nice letter about him. He said what a fine boy he had been, how well liked — such a grand letter. She's kept it ever since, that, and the telegram. Then she had this boy a few months later and brought him up all by herself. He went through Loyola too. And he was just like his father — smart as a whip. At the top of his class. We clapped and clapped at his graduation. He won so many prizes! He kept going up for one after the other. It got to be almost funny. She was so proud of him. And such a good-looking boy. He had his whole life ahead of him. Oh, it's so tragic! How can I face his mother? Maybe this principal of Loyola will write her a letter about him too. Oh, I'm sure he will. He was such a nice boy. Everybody liked him. He was the apple of her eye. What can I say to her? Thank God the priest will be there. I'll phone some of our friends when I get there. All I can do is put my arms around her. What is there to say? If she wants to talk, I'll listen. I'll make something for everyone to eat. I'll phone my daughters at work and get them to come to her place right away. Maybe I'll get some of his friends to come over. Or maybe that would be too hard on her. We'll say the Rosary. Oh, my God, here's my stop. I don't know what I'm going to say to her."

"I'm sorry," I said.

She touched my hand, said, "Thank you, dear. Goodbye," and got off the car.

172

Official Army Casualties

OTTAWA, Feb. 1—The Canadian (Active) Army issues its 783rd casualty list of the war as follows:

OFFICERS
WOUNDED
Eastern Ontario Regiment
FORSYTH-SMITH, Charles Maxwell, Lieut., Wolfville, N.S.

INJURED
Nova Scotia and P.E.I. Regiment
ALLEN, Thomas Leslie, Capt., Halifax, N.S.

PREVIOUSLY REPORTED MISSING NOW REPORTED PRISONER OF WAR
Regiment de Quebec
CHARETTE, Jean Paul Théodore, Lieut., Ottawa.
PLOUFFE, Joseph Orphila Fanaida, Lieut., Mrs. Rose Emma Plouffe, (mother), 5811 Louis Hebert St., Montreal, Que.
VALLEE, Marie Francois Pierre, Capt., Quebec, Que.
Nova Scotia and P.E.I. Regiment
CAMPBELL, Samuell Fraser, Lieut., New Glasgow, N.S.
RHODENIZER, Leon Merrill, Major, New Glasgow, N.S.
TRAINOR, Joseph Austin, Capt., Truro, N.S.
New Brunswick Regiment
LANGILLE, Roland Alexander, Lieut., Tatamagouche, N.S.
SMITH, Gerald Albert Percy, Lieut., Lower Newcastle, N.B.

WARRANT OFFICERS, N.C.O.s AND MEN
PREVIOUSLY REPORTED MISSING NOW FOR OFFICIAL PURPOSES PRESUMED KILLED IN ACTION
Royal Canadian Corps of Signals
HILT, George Everette, Sigmn., D24230, Mrs. Grita Dorothy Hilt (wife), 2544 St. Antoine St., Montreal, Que.
Eastern Ontario Regiment
FREEBURN, Percy Angus Neil Alexander, Pte., Flinton, Ont.

KILLED IN ACTION
Royal Canadian Artillery
BRADFORD, Gerald Anderson, Gnr., Eastons Corners, Ont.
NASON, George Arthur, L/Bdr., Oromocto, N.B.
WATERMAN, Guy Victor, Sgt., K76995, Mrs. Angeline D. L. Waterman (wife), 1560 St. Zotique St E., Montreal 35, Que.
Eastern Ontario Regiment
GAGNON, Joseph Roger, Pte., Hull, Que.
Quebec Regiment
JEFFREY, Arthur Francis, L/Cpl., D81816, Mrs. Elenor L. Jeffrey (wife), 2451 Coleraine St., Point St. Charles, Montreal, Que.
Nova Scotia and P.E.I. Regiment
WITHERALL, Benjamin James, Pte., North Sydney, N.S.
New Brunswick Regiment
ANDREW, Ian Barnes, Rfn., Saint John, N.B.

Quebec Regiment
DUFOUR, Marc, Cpl., D71829, Mrs. Gracia Dufour (mother), 108 Daly Ave., Ottawa.
Nova Scotia and P.E.I. Regiment
BATT, Frederick Robert, Pte., Halifax, N.S.
New Brunswick Regiment
SAULNIER, Pascal, Pte., Memramcook E., N.B.

SEVERELY WOUNDED
Nova Scotia and P.E.I. Regiment
STEELE, Louis Joseph, Pte., Gaspereaux, P.E.I.
New Brunswick Regiment
STEWART, Eugene Malcolm, L/Cpl., Chipman, N.B.
Manitoba Regiment
BRIDEAU, Vincent, Pte., Tilley Road, N.B.

WOUNDED
Royal Canadian Artillery
McDOUGALL, Angus, Gnr., North Sydney, N.S.
Quebec Regiment
ANTLE, Reginald, Pte., St. John, Newfoundland.
Regiment de Quebec
METHOT, Ferdinand, Cpl., E12118, Nazaire Methot (Father), Apt.5, 323 Ontario E., Montreal 18, Que.
Nova Scotia and P.E.I. Regiment
GRANT, Harold Edwin, Pte., Londonderry, N.S.
HARRINGTON, Arthur Gerald, Cpl., Greenwich, N.S.
JOLLIMORE, Robert Ainsley Pte., Terence Bay, N.S.
Canadian Forestry Corps
ELLARD, Orval Claude, L/Cpl., Wright, Que.

SLIGHTLY WOUNDED
Canadian Armoured Corps
McCARTHY, John Francis, Tpr., Montague, P.E.I.
Eastern Ontario Regiment
RUNIONS, Arthur Gordon, Sgt., Cornwall, Ont.
Regiment de Quebec
ALLARD, Romeo, Pte., Lac au Saumon, Que.
BEAUDRY, Fernand, Pte., D106147, Edmond Beaudry (father), 668 Boulevard Perras, Ahuntsic, Montreal, Que.
LABERGE, Paul Pte., Riviere du Sud, Que.
LEPAGE, Claude, Pte., Quebec, Que.
Nova Scotia and P.E.I. Regiment
HAYES, Patrick Francis, Pte., Sydney, N.S.
KAVANAGH, Ronald Thomas, Pte., Glace Bay, N.S.

WOUNDED REMAINING ON DUTY
Regiment de Quebec
DUGUAY, Aurele, Pte., Shelter Bay, Que.

WOUNDED (ACCIDENTALLY)
Canadian Armoured Corps
GILLAN, John James, Tpr., D128716, James E. Gillan (father), Peake Station, P.E.I.

DIED OF WOUNDS
Quebec Regiment
CHATTERTON, Gordon, Pte., New Carlisle, Que.
Regiment de Quebec
FORTIN, Georges David, Sgt., Ste. Marie de Beauce, Que.
New Brunswick Regiment
COUGHLAN, Kenneth James, Sgt., Barnettville, N.B.
MERRITT, Neale Warren, Pte., Cross Creek, N.B.
Royal Canadian Army Service Corps
NORRIS, Herbert William, L/Cpl., C122218, Mrs. Bettie I. Norris (Wife), 1002 Allard Ave., Verdun, Que.

PREVIOUSLY REPORTED MISSING NOW REPORTED DIED WHILE PRISONER OF WAR
Quebec Regiment
JOHNSTON, Gerald MacIntosh, Pte., D81740, Mrs. Clara Maud Johnston (Mother), 205 E. 78th St., Apt. 11E, New York. N.Y., U.S.A.

PREVIOUSLY REPORTED MISSING NOW REPORTED DIED (DROWNED)
Eastern Ontario Regiment
HALL, James Samuel, Pte., Algonquin, Ont.

DANGEROUSLY WOUNDED
Royal Canadian Artillery
VEALE, Stanley Albert, Gnr., D7134, Albert H. Veale (Father), c/o Massey Harris Co., Woodstock, Ont.
Quebec Regiment
ASCH, Clifford Maxwell, Pte., D143297, Michael Asch (Father), 3482 Northcliffe Ave., Montreal 28, Que.

SERIOUSLY WOUNDED
Royal Canadian Artillery
BRUNET, Raymond Joseph, Gnr., Eastview, Ont.

INJURED
Royal Canadian Artillery
MAXAM, Alfred Francis, Gnr., Ottawa.
Royal Canadian Ordnance Corps
FITZHERBERT, Lloyd George, Pte., Fredericton, N.B.

SLIGHTLY INJURED
Royal Canadian Artillery
LAGUEUX, Benoit, Gnr., D118626, Mrs. Alice Lagueux (mother), Box 202, Hearst, Ont.
VALLEAU, Gordon Drummond, Sgt., Kingston, Ont. (Wife overseas.)
Quebec Regiment
PORTER, Robert William, Pte., D81885, Mrs. Jessie Porter (mother), 1063 Beaver Hall Hill, Montreal 1, Que.
Regiment de Quebec
NADEAU, Real, Pte., Les Etroits, Que.
Nova Scotia and P.E.I. Regiment
BOWER, Howard Allison, Cpl., Aylesford, N.S.
Royal Canadian Army Service Corps
LANDRY, Bruno Joseph, Pte., D115472, Mrs. Diana Y. Landry (wife), 5228 6th Ave., Rosemont, Montreal, Que.

AIR FORCE CASUALTIES

Ottawa, June 4. — (P) — The R.C.A.F. issued today its 900th casualty list of the war, containing 24 names and including two men killed on active service overseas and 11 men missing on active service after air operations overseas.

Following is the latest list of casualties, with official numbers and next-of-kin:

OVERSEAS:

KILLED ON ACTIVE SERVICE:

Bandur, Sigmund Bernard, Flt.-Sgt., R171571, Barney Bandur (father). Broderick, Sask.

Hills, Keith Alexander, FO, J12985, J. C. Hills (father), Tara, Ont.

MISSING ON ACTIVE SERVICE AFTER AIR OPERATIONS:

Barnes, Arthur John George, Flt.-Sgt., R157147, W. G. Barnes (father), St. James, Man.

Burrows, John Woolatt, FO. J22599, H. R. Burrows (father), 163 Portland avenue, Town of Mount Royal, Que.

Doyle, Kevin Joseph, Flt.-Sgt., R157-883, James Doyle (father), Vancouver.

Driver, Paul Edward, PO, J85612, T. H. Driver (father), Toronto.

Easen, Richard Frederick, Flt.-Sgt., R163503, F. A. Essen (father), Keene, Ont.

McCoy, Daniel Albert, PO, J35666, Mrs. D. A. McCoy (wife), Seattle, Washington.

McDonald, Donald, PO, J85613 Angus McDonald (father), Goderich, Ont.

Smythe, James Ethelred, Sgt., R190191, H. H. Smythe (father), St. Stephen, N.B.

Whaley, Harold Harvey, PO, J18716, Mrs. Stuart Gellander (mother), Leamington, Ont.

PREVIOUSLY REPORTED MISSING ON ACTIVE SERVICE — NOW FOR OFFICIAL PURPOSES PRESUMED DEAD:

Gardiner, Raymond, D.F.C., Flt.-Lt., J15548, Mrs. Raymond Gardiner (wife), Elmwood, Ont. z

Fairweather, Edgar Lloyd, PO, J21535, Major V. W. Fairweather (father), Sun Life Building, Montreal.

Haugen, Willard Melvin, Flt.-Sgt., R114914, O. N. Haugen (father), Strongfield, Sask.

Kay, Gordon Harry, FO., J23845, Mrs G. H. Kay (wife), Toronto.

Kavanaugh, Joseph Garnet Stewart, WO, R67163, Mrs. G. E. Kavanaugh (mother), Cardiffal, Ont.

Leake, Albert Edward, Flt.-Sgt., R93208, Mrs. A. E. Leake (wife), Toronto.

McIntyre, Harry Starkey, FO, J7418, Section Officer K. L. McIntyre (wife), Saskatoon, Sask.

Odell, James Gilmour, PO, J19278, W. H. Odell, K.C. (father), Wetaskiwin, Alta.

Shann, Harry Pritchard, FO, J21901, Mrs. Fred Shann (mother), Flint, Mich.

Stinson, Harley Vernon, PO, J19157, O. W. Stinson (father), St. Andrews, N.B.

SERIOUSLY INJURED ON ACTIVE SERVICE:

Hancock, Royce William, LAC, R143045, S. C. Hancock (father), North Vancouver, B.C.

CANADIANS IN THE ROYAL AIR FORCE OVERSEAS:

KILLED ON ACTIVE SERVICE:

Motherwell, David, Flt.-Sgt., GB143-7121, Wren Betty Schacter, W954, Deep Brook, N.S.

MISSING ON ACTIVE SERVICE AFTER AIR OPERATIONS:

Nelson, D. H., PO, RAF54296, Mrs. M. F. Nelson (mother), New Westminster, B.C.

CANADIAN NAVY CASUALTIES

Ottawa, June 4—(P)—The Royal Canadian Navy issued Saturday its 249th casualty list of the war, containing three names and reporting two men killed in action overseas and one dead of injuries suffered overseas.

Following is the latest list of casualties, with official numbers and next-of-kin:

KILLED IN ACTION OVERSEAS MAY 23

Evans, Donald Lewis, OS., V62018, William G. Evans (father), Saint John, N.B.

Allison, Charles Herbert, AB., V34897, Mrs. Jennie May Allison (mother), Trenton, Ont.

DIED AS THE RESULT OF SERIOUS INJURIES SUFFERED OVERSEAS MAY 23

Mason, Charles Roy, LS., 3884, William Mason (father), Vancouver.

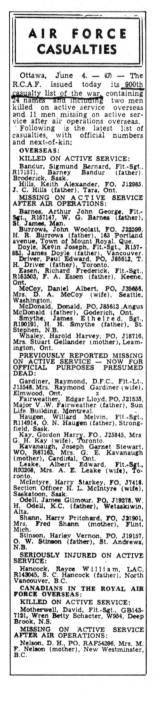

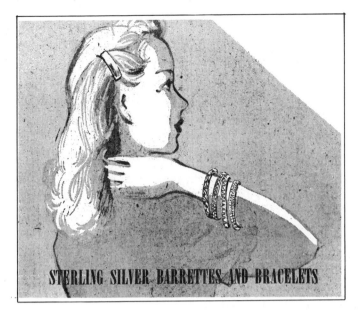
STERLING SILVER BARRETTES AND BRACELETS

CHAPTER TWENTY-SEVEN

FASHION FADDISTS

"We call the bookkeeper 'the Ette', Nancy had explained to me as we ate lunch in the stockroom on the first day of my job at the insurance brokers.

"The 'Ette'? How come?"

"Because he's so small — like a miniature man, or manette. As in kitchenette or roomette."

The bookkeeper was the only man sharing the office with the other four girls, Muriel, Nancy, Suzanne, Michelle, and me. The company's executives, all middle-aged men, occupied the individual offices that fanned out from our larger one. The Ette's desk was at the front of the office, facing a wall. We all sat behind him, pounding on our typewriters.

It was unfortunate for him that a 1945 fashion fad was to wear as many sterling silver bracelets as you could afford.

"Eaton's has a sale of sterling silver bracelets at a dollar a-piece," Suzanne reported one day after an uptown shopping trip on her lunch hour.

The next Saturday we all stocked up. The following Monday, the five of us sat behind the Ette, our arms encircled with bracelets. When we were all typing at once, the jangling of our bracelets set up such a racket, the poor man hunched his shoulders and ducked his head, in a vain attempt to withdraw from the noise.

No one girl was the fashion trend-setter. We all made our contributions. I, for instance, was responsible for two trends.

It was the year of Revlon's "Pink Period", when they introduced their line of nail polishes and lipsticks with names like Pink Garter, Pink Lightning, Mrs. Miniver Rose, and Rosy Future. I bought one of their lipsticks and wore it one day. It made a hit with all four girls.

"What's that color?" one of them asked.

"Revlon's Pink Lightning," I said.

The next day they were all wearing it.

My other contribution was made when Bob gave me a cologne by Harriet Hubbard Ayer called Pink Clover. They all liked its fragrance, and soon the whole office smelled of it.

One morning when Muriel sat down beside me, I said, "Nice tan."

"It's not a tan. It's Overglo," she said.

"Gee, it looks just like a tan," I marvelled.

Within a week we all had Overglo tans.

Our hair was worn long and held back either with a sterling silver barrette, or a black velvet band sewn to a piece of elastic that was hidden under our hair.

One day, Mr. MacEwan, one of the executives, an absent-minded type said to me, "Muriel, will you come into my office, please. I have a few letters to dictate."

"I'm not Muriel," I said, "I'm Mary."

"Oh, sorry," he said, then turned to Nancy and said, "Muriel, I have a few letters to get out."

"I'm not Muriel," Nancy said, "I'm Nancy."

"Oh," the poor man said, "Excuse me," and retreated to his office.

He must have thought, "They look the same, and they smell the same, how am I supposed to tell the difference?"

When he was out of sight, Nancy and I smiled at each other with our Pink Lightninged mouths.

Lucky for us, it wasn't considered unpatriotic for office girls to wear their hair long, as it was for war workers. Actress Veronica Lake was one of the people responsible for the popularity of long hair. Not only did she wear her hair long, but she wore it covering one eye. This peekaboo hairdo was copied by twenty thousand women who operated turret lathes and stamp presses in war plants. Thus, the average female war worker operated at 50% reduced visual efficiency. Or, she had, as

176

Dickens described Mr. Squeers in *Nicholas Nickleby*, "but one eye, and the popular prejudice runs in favor of two."

After too many incidents of these women catching their long hair in machinery and scalping themselves, the U.S. Government declared Veronica Lake a menace to the war effort. The War Man-Power Commission then contacted the War Production Board (the counterpart of Canada's Wartime Prices And Trade Board) which in turn got in touch with Paramount Pictures, which took up the matter with Veronica Lake, who said that from then on she'd be happy to wear her hair on top of her head. She hadn't liked wearing her hair over one eye in the first place.

We had an added interest in Veronica Lake because she had attended the Villa Marie convent in Montreal.

The long hair fad also gave rise to another fashion item — the snood. It was headgear somewhat like a hairnet, only produced in a wider mesh and a variety of colors. None of us office girls wore them, considering them too ugly. When snoods first came on the scene, my mother told me that in her day they had been called "fascinators" — certainly a more attractive sounding name than snood.

Another popular fashion item for women in 1945, was the Eisenhower jacket, patterned after the windbreaker battle jacket worn by General "Ike", which in turn had been patterned after the official British battle-dress. It was the same as the RCAF battle jacket that Bob had worn.

We girls must have looked like some exotic branch of the military as we showed up for work in our plaid Eisenhower jackets, and colorful Montgomery berets.

As the war progressed, and more and more people came to depend on bicycles for transportation, pedal-pushers — knee-length shorts — were introduced so that, according to LIFE magazine, college girls wouldn't catch their pantlegs in their bicycle chains. Why college girls' pantlegs were more vulnerable to the teeth of bicycle chains than anyone else's was not explained.

Nylon stockings had no sooner been introduced in May of 1940, than they became a scarce commodity. (Du Pont giveth, and Du Pont taketh away). This was due to the nylon yarn being needed for parachute cloth. To compensate, stockings of lacy mesh, popcorn stitch, and ribbed cotton were brought out in various colors.

When summer came, leg lotions were de rigueur. "It looks like nylon," Ogilvy's ad for leg make-up proclaimed. It didn't. The kind that Cath, Mitt, Wooly, and I bought was called Duration Leg Do.

177

One brow-wiper of a night, when the humidity made Montreal as hot and damp as a Louisiana bayou, Wooly and I double-dated with Bob and her current boyfriend, Huzzie. Despite the heat, we went to a dance at the Y. Wooly and I had dutifully applied our Duration Do in the afternoon, but hadn't taken into account that the hot night would make us sweat.

When we were out on the dance floor, Wooly leaned over and hissed, "Don't look now, but your legs are running." I immediately looked down and saw that I had brown and biege striped legs. A glance at hers revealed that they were chipmunk striped as well. We spent some time in the ladies room trying to repair the damage with wet paper towels, but even so, for the rest of the evening we looked like victims of some rare skin disease.

Reversible coats were a big item in the 1940s. They were two coats in one, in that worn on one side, the coat was a raincoat, and on the other, it was an ordinary spring coat. The idea, presumably, was that if you were wearing the coat tweed or camel hair side out, and it should suddenly start to rain, you would immediately peel it off and reverse it to the raincoat side. But then you would have the side that had been rained on next to you. Well, maybe if you were lucky, you would perceive that it was going to rain before leaving home, and you would reverse it before going outside. Anyway, it was very popular.

Movies seldom set fashion trends — film costume designers tended to follow rather than lead — but the first time I ever saw a shoulder purse worn by a civilian was when Signe Hasso used one in the 1945 spy thriller, "The House On 92nd Street". My first thought when I saw it was how practical it would be for a foreign correspondent. I could wear one over my shoulder and have my hands free to carry a portable typewriter and a travelling bag.

In the men's fashion department, things had quieted down. The zoot suit ensemble seemed to no longer enrage servicemen as it once had.

In Montreal, the zoot suit war had probably seen its greatest skirmishes back in the spring and summer of 1944.

Battles between armed forces personnel and zoot suiters were waged in Verdun, Rosemount, La Fontaine Park, and on Ste. Catherine Street. In dancehalls, night-clubs, and restaurants, as well as on the street, servicemen and zoot suiters wounded each other with clubs, knives, fists, and broken bottles. These fights were broken up by steel-helmeted Provincial Police, the Navy Shore Patrol and the Army Provost Corps..

Participants were either arrested, hospitalized, or taken into custody by the Military Police.

But by 1945, a more benign attitude was adopted toward zoot suits and their wearers. One reason may have been that in New York City a new type of jazz was a-borning. Called bebop, it involved the flatting of fifths.

Its most visible proponent was a musician named Dizzy Gillespie who had played in Cab Calloway's band at one point. Perhaps the outrageousness of Calloway's outfit appealed to him, because many of his listeners considered his new music outrageous. In any case, Gillespie adopted the fashion style as well, and by so doing, dissipated all of the animosity toward it. It just became an amusing way for the bop musicians to set themselves apart from their fellow musicmakers.

But while the zoot suit war was engaged on the home front, it was not one of tolerance or fashion's finest hours. With all its social and racial overtones it was essentially the confrontation between men who had volunteered to fight for their country and those, although young and fit enough to fight, who had not.

Forty Arrested, Scores Injured In Sailors and Zoot-suiters Riots

An island-wide armed forces campaign against zoot-suiters reached new heights Saturday night as scattered battles in Verdun and in the heart of Montreal brought injuries to scores of persons and the arrest of more than 40, most of them sailors.

From mid-evening until early yesterday morning the rioting exploded in dancehalls, restaurants, night clubs and on the street, with clubs, knives, broken bottles and other weapons everywhere in evidence.

Pitched battles have reached such dangerous proportions that police have been ordered on emergency schedules in several municipalities, while squads of provincial traffic officers with motorcycles and cars were lined up outside headquarters last night in preparation for possible new disturbances.

Lafontaine Park saw a stormy 45-minute session last night as soldiers and zoot-suiters staged several brief struggles. Police said about 100 soldiers were involved and that several "drape-shape" youths had their clothing ripped. Hundreds of citizens who had gathered at the park to hear an outdoor concert hampered police efforts but control of the situation was gained without serious injuries being reported.

Steel-helmeted provincial policemen were among the emergency squads kept on call last night in case of out-of-town trouble, and two truckloads of burly Naval Shore Patrol men patrolled St. Catherine street.

Police timed the battles as starting in earnest shortly before 10 p.m. Saturday, and by the time they and squads of sailors from the Navy Shore Patrol had the situation under control around 2.30 a.m. yesterday 38 servicemen and two civilians had been arrested and three sailors, two civilians and a police constable had been taken to hospital. In addition to those actually arrested, the shore patrol took scores of other sailors in custody and these were handed over to naval authorities.

Of those arrested by police, 36 were sailors, one a soldier and one an airman. All were charged with fighting and disturbing the peace. They were released to naval authorities yesterday morning but will face charges in Recorder's Court today.

A serious view of the fighting was taken by Ottawa, where an official navy statement last night said a full inquiry would be made into the rioting and circumstances surrounding it.

No information was available here or at Ottawa as to the whereabouts of those sailors arrested and later released in custody of their superiors, where the sailors who rioted were from nor how so many hundreds of them were able to gather in the centre of the city.

Promise of investigation into the battles came from high naval authorities and was announced by an official navy spokesman.

"A full inquiry is being held," the spokesman said, but added that "no statement" would be made until that inquiry had been completed.

CHAPTER TWENTY-EIGHT

WE WON! WE WON!

Imagine a city whose football team wins the Grep Cup; whose hockey team wins the Stanley Cup; and whose baseball team wins the pennant — All on the Very Same Day — and you have a small idea of what May 7th, 1945 was like in Montreal.

On Saturday, April 28th, there was a newsflash on the radio that Germany had surrendered, and in certain cities, Montreal being one, there were premature victory celebrations in the streets until the report was officially denied by President Truman, successor to FDR, who had died on April 12th.

But from that time on there was a feeling of optimism in the air. Every day on our lunch hour, one of us in the office went over to look at *The Montreal Star*'s outdoor giant bulletin board to read the latest news, then report back to the others.

On May 6th there was another report that the Germans had surrendered, and that, too, was denied. So our mood when we came to work on May 7th, while optimistic and anticipatory, was slightly skeptical. We had no urge to make a third trip down the garden path.

We had no sooner settled at our desks than we heard the roar go up outside. Racing to the windows, we looked down and saw people on St.

James Street cheering and raising their arms jubilantly in victory salutes. Office workers in the buildings across from us started to throw ticker-tape out of their windows onto the street below. Not to be outdone by the stockbrokers, we rushed to our stock room to get the rolls of paper that were used in the adding machines, and unrolled them to make streamers. The Ette opened the window, and we contributed our bit to the blanket of paper starting to cover the street.

Within a few minutes, our boss arrived, grinning and slapping his hands together, saying, "I just read it on the Star bulletin board — unconditional surrender!" We all squealed as if we had needed an eyewitness account to confirm it for us. The other executives came out of their offices, and there was a lot of hugging and handshaking all around.

Mr. MacEwan had a son in the Navy, and Mr. Filion had a son in the Army, and they clapped each other on the shoulders saying happily, "Our boys are safe." I felt the same about Choate. Even though he was overseas, he was no longer in danger, and would be able to come home and see his baby girl at last.

"You girls might as well go home," our boss said. "There won't be any work done today anyway." So we rushed out to join the din below where steamboat whistles were blowing, church bells ringing, and auto horns honking. The people in the office building above were hurling down tickertape, toilet paper, and confetti on us. Some street revellers hung the tickertape around their necks like scarfs.

Men appeared from nowhere, selling flags. We bought some, and waved them as we tried to make our way along St. James Street and up Beaver Hall Hill to Ste. Catherine Street. Everyone was happy and in wonderfully high spirits — smiling, laughing, cheering, yelling, dancing, hugging, kissing, singing.

Traffic came to a standstill as the streets filled with thousands of celebrants. No one was drunk in the early hours after the announcement. One reason being that it was early in the day and the taverns hadn't opened, and the other, that Premier Maurice Duplessis had issued the edict that the minute the war ended, the sale of alcohol was to stop for 48 hours, even if the drink had already been ordered, or the beer was in the process of passing from the grocer's hands to the hands of the customer.

The effort to make our way uphill through the throngs was like trying to swim through a river of glue. In the air was the sound of ambulance sirens and fire engines clanging, due to false alarms being set off. Conga lines snaked through the crowds, impeding our progress all the more. Boys in uniform were taking advantage of the light-hearted mood by trying to get girls to kiss them. Some of the girls were obliging, others weren't. People were flashing V for Victory signs with their fingers, and waving their flags over their heads.

We eventually made it to Phillips Square on Ste. Catherine Street — a scene of great activity. A platform had been set up for the Eighth Victory Loan Drive, and recorded music was being played over the loudspeakers. Teenage boys and girls danced; teenage girls danced together; and groups of merry-makers joined hands, formed circles, and just ran around to the music. The Andrews' Sisters singing "Rum And Coca-Cola" cut through the din. I said goodbye to the others and started heading along Ste. Catherine Street to try to get to Peate Musical on Mansfield.

Morgan's, Eaton's and Simpson's Department stores were all closed, and as I turned up Mansfield, Bob and his brother had just locked up Peate's. I joined them and we walked up Mansfield to the garage where their cars were parked.

Once Bob and I were in his car and turning from Mansfield onto Sherbrooke Street, we found it was the same story. Crowds were jammed into the street, and we had to inch through them because they were in no hurry to part just so that we could drive through. That was okay because we were in no hurry to drive through anyway. It was such a lark to be among so many happy, laughing people. A block away were the Roddick Gates which led onto the McGill campus. We weren't aware of it at the time, but inside some of the buildings, McGill students were writing final exams, and were expected to ignore the jubilation outside and finish them before joining the celebrations. What superhuman willpower they had to have had.

As we drove, we turned on the car radio to listen to the CBC Victory broadcast, and heard our fellow Montrealers cheering over the radio on a program that was being broadcast all over the world.

After driving at a snail's pace, we managed to arrive at Bob's home in Westmount. Several members of his family were there, and though his mother hadn't been expecting all of us, there was more than enough food for any number of unexpected guests. It seemed almost biblical to me, like the miracle of the loaves and fishes.

Though she had lived in Westmount since the age of four, Bob's mother still spoke with a British accent, and while we were eating she said excitedly, "Just imagine how Churchill and their majesties must be feeling now!" That thought made us pause to regret that FDR hadn't lived to celebrate the day too.

It wasn't until the next day that we began to hear stories of how some people had chosen to celebrate the day.

Mitt reported that she had dropped in on the festivities at Heller's in the afternoon.

Heller's was a logical place for VE Day celebrants to congregate because it was the unofficial home base of N.D.G. teenaged boys who had joined the services.

Up on the wall, just as you came in the door, was a posterboard bearing the names of Heller habitués who were in the armed forces. "Ma" Heller referred to them as "my boys" because she had been serving them cherry Cokes, sodas, and Black and White sundaes for years. When they were shipped overseas, she kept up a steady correspondence with them, and sent them parcels of chocolate bars and cigarettes.

It seemed that the majority of the Heller's gang that we knew had joined the Navy, and had served on destroyers and corvettes from the mid-Atlantic to the icy North Atlantic. But Heller's and N.D.G., and Westmount, and all of Montreal as well as the rest of Canada had been well represented in all theaters of this global war.

More than a thousand Canadian airman had participated in the 1,000 plane raid on Cologne. They had led the deadly attack on Dieppe which some said served as a rehearsal for the Normandy invasion. Some 5,000 Canadians, 1,000 British and 50 Americans took part in the raid and more than half were killed, wounded or taken prisoner. Along with British and American troops they had invaded Sicily and Italy to crush Mussilini and beat back the Germans hill by hill and town by town and street by street. They had taken part in the D Day landing. There were over 1,000 casualties at Juno Beach alone. They then fought their way through France and played a major role in the liberation of Holland. Indeed Canadians had been involved in battles for far away places with names ranging from Apeldoorn to Zeebrugge.

"Pa" Heller never tried to compete with his wife's generosity. He did often say however, that on the day the war in Europe ended, he would stand everyone to a free Coke.

Mitt said the place was packed. Pa Heller bustled around the soda fountain, and the ting of the cash register sounded each time he rang up another Coke sale. When Mitt said, "Hey, Pa, I though this was the day when Cokes would be on the house." Pa replied excitedly, "On such a happy day, do *I* know what I'm doing?"

The next day, May 8th, the day that was officially named VE Day and designated for celebration, was much more quiet and orderly, except for what happened in Nova Scotia.

The city of Halifax was described the day after VE Day as looking the way it had on the day of the Halifax explosion during the First World War. Two buildings were burned and gutted; the windows of all the stores in the business district were smashed; and the contents of the stores looted — particularly the liquor stores. All this was said to be the result of rioting servicemen wreaking "vengeance" or "protest" against the way they had allegedly been treated by landlords and merchants during their posting in Halifax. The damage was estimated at a million dollars.

Celebrations elsewhere in Canada on VE Day were more subdued, taking the form of thanksgiving services in churches, parks, and at the Great War Memorials in city squares.

In London, the Brits forgot their customary reserve, and went wild. Maybe one difference was that there the Pubs were open until they ran dry. Of course, they had been "in" the war. The Germans had tried to bomb London out of existence and failed. The British had a lot to celebrate. Thousands gathered in Piccadilly Circus and sang "There'll Always Be An England"; the King, Queen, and two princesses appeared several times on the balcony of Buckingham Palace to deafening cheers from the crowds below. And fifty thousand people crowded in Whitehall to join Winston Churchill in singing, "Land of Hope and Glory". What a moment that must have been!

When Churchill addressed the crowd he said, "God bless us all. This is your victory! It is the victory of the cause of freedom in every land. In all our long history we have never seen a greater day than this. Everyone, man or woman, has done their best. Everyone has tried. Neither the long years, nor the dangers, nor the fierce attacks of the enemy, have in any way weakened the independent resolve of the British nation. God bless you all."

Montreal Star May 7, 1945

Salute to Victory!

Through blood, through sweat, through tears——his the inspiration

CHAPTER TWENTY-NINE

"EACH MAN SAID A 'MY GOD' "

Because I always gauged the importance of a news story by the size of the type used in the headline, I saw that the big news on Monday, August 6, 1945, as gleaned from the banner headline on the front page of *The Montreal Star* was: DOMINION-PROVINCIAL TALKS COMMENCE.

A fairly small headline read: "U.S. Drops Atomic Bomb On Japs". Then in smaller type, "President Truman Reveals New Weapon; Has Power Equal to 20,000 Tons of TNT". I had no idea what the power of 1,000 tons of TNT might be, so the power of 20,000 tons was equally elusive.

The British United Press story began:

> President Truman today announced that an "atomic bomb" has been used against Japan for the first time with power equal to 20,000 tons of TNT.
>
> In a statement issued at the White House Mr. Truman revealed that 16 hours ago — sometime Sunday — an American airplane dropped one of the bombs on Hiroshima, an important Japanese army base.

187

The news made hardly a ripple on radio newscasts either. It wasn't until the next day that the full significance of the event began to come out. The Tuesday August 7th Star's banner headline proclaimed:

TOKYO APPALLED BY ATOMIC BOMB

Hiroshima Devastation Still Not Fully Known

Japs Say Few Missiles Fell; Dust Cloud Still Obscures Area

It was apparent from the news story that the Japanese had no idea what had hit them. For one thing they believed that several B29 Super-fortresses had dropped several bombs. (How else could so much devastation have been wrought?) But in fact there had been one plane and one bomb.

So far no pictures had been taken because the first photograph planes to reach the Hiroshima area after the raid were unable (according to the B.U.P.) to penetrate the dense dust and smoke rising from the stricken area.

The first recorded Japanese reference to the bomb had come over Tokyo radio. The Domei agency broadcast that:

> "Tokyo, August 7 — President Harry Truman and Prime Minister Clement Attlee announced simultaneously yesterday that American aircraft on Sunday afternoon (United States time) dropped an 'atomic bomb' on Hiroshima, according to United Press and Reuters newscasts recorded here."

Though the Japanese were still ignorant of the bomb that had been dropped on them, North American newspaper readers were told that it had the power to blind persons within a five-mile radius, and to kill within four miles. Its searing blast was said to fuse the earth into silicate-like formations.

The Star's August 7th editorial quoted a cautionary statement made by former British Prime Minster Winston Churchill on August 6th, the day the bomb was dropped:

> "This revelation of the secrets of Nature, long mercifully withheld from man, should arouse the most solemn reflections in the mind and conscience of every human being capable of comprehension. We must, indeed, pray that these awful agencies will be made to

conduct peace among nations and that instead of wreaking measure-
less havoc upon the entire globe they may become a perennial fountain of world prosperity."

On Wednesday August 8th, more was known. The Star's banner
headline read:

MOST OF HIROSHIMA ERASED BY ATOM BOMB
Tokyo Acknowledges 'Indescribable Power'
Unofficial U.S. Sources Set Casualty Toll at 100,000

The U.P. Story quoted a Tokyo broadcast that said:

"The impact of the bomb was so terrific that practically all living
things, human and animal, were literally seared to death by the
tremendous heat and pressure engendered by the blast."

Another page one story gave an eye-witness account from the men
who dropped the bomb. Col. Paul W. Tibbets Jr., the 36 year old pilot of
the Superfortress called the *Enola Gay* that flew the mission said,

"It was hard to believe what we saw.
"Below us, rising rapidly, was a tremendous black cloud. Nothing
was visible where only minutes before the outline of the city with
its streets and buildings and waterfront piers was clearly apparent.
"It happened so fast we couldn't see anything and could only feel
the heat from the flash and concussion from the blast."

Capt. William Parsons, U.S.N. described it this way:

"There was a terrific flash of light — even in the daytime visual
shock was apparent from several miles.
"That was the first indication I had that the bomb worked. Each man
said a... 'My God'.
"What had been Hiroshima was going up in a mountain of smoke.
"First I could see a mushroom of boiling dust — apparently with
some debris in it — up to 20,000 feet. The boiling continued three
or four minutes as I watched.
"Then a white cloud plumed upward from the center to some 40,000
feet. An angry dust cloud spread all around the city.
"There were small fires on the fringes of the city, apparently burning as buildings crumbled and the gas mains broke."

As soon as the first atomic bomb was dropped on Japan, President Truman demanded that the Japanese surrender, with the threat that more such bombs would follow. But the Japanese refused.

On Thursday, August 9th, an even more potent atomic bomb was dropped, this time on the city of Nagasaki.

On August 15th, Emperor Hirohito spoke on the radio for the very first time to his one hundred million subjects, saying that the atomic bomb had forced Japan to accept the first military defeat in the 2,605 years of her history. It was the first time that any Japanese had ever heard the voice of the Emperor, other than a few government and military officials and members of the Royal family.

How could his subjects be certain that it was in fact their Emperor speaking, and not an imposter? He used the Royal "we", which no other person in Japan was permitted to do. So in awe of him were his subjects, that whenever he appeared in public, they did not dare to look at him. So his making such an announcement on the radio must have had a profound effect on them.

The VJ Day didn't have the same impact for Bob and me as VE Day had — the reason being that we were at a lake in the Adirondacks when the word of the surrender was broadcast at 7 p.m. on August 14th.

It was pouring rain when we first heard the news, and Bob and I toyed with the idea of driving to one of the nearest towns — Malone, Saranac Lake, Lake Placid, or Plattsburgh, to join in the celebrations, but it would have meant crossing the lake in the heavy rain to get to the garage so we decided against it.

The next morning, at first light, we heard the gunning of outboard motors. People had decked out their boats with flags and bunting and were going up and down the lake calling out joyfully. Bob and I hopped into his boat and joined the parade.

"No more gas rationing," one fellow shouted to us, and gunned his motor all the harder.

Bob waved and gunned his own motor in reply, then said to me, "Hey, that's right. No more of a lot of things. Like no more import restrictions on musical instruments!" He gunned his motor again.

"No more 'just one to a customer' signs," I said.

VAROOM

"No more synthetic rubber tires."

VAROOM

"No more beat-up typewriters."

VAROOM.

190

"No more 'priorities'."

VAROOM.

Back at the house we listened to radio reports of the celebrations going on all over North America.

Between news reports and commentaries, the radio played songs like "We'll Meet Again" and "It's Been A Long, Long Time".

Had it ever. Six long years! That day back in September of 1939 when Britain declared war on Germany and Cath and I were talking about the possibility of Canada going to war, who would have thought then that it would be such a long, long time?

Horrors of Osviecin Death Camp Related by Doctor Who Escaped

Grisly Murder Area Where Four Million Non-Aryans Were Burned and Tortured to Death by Nazis Recalled by Czech Interviewed Here

By RON MARSH

Each daybreak at Osviecin extermination camp the guards would line about 100 prisoners. Some of the prisoners would be Russian officers, some Polish civilians and some of them would be Jews. The Russians tried to hold themselves straight. The Poles and the Jews were past caring how they stood. The faces of the prisoners were spotted with the red rash of typhus.

Each morning after he had breakfasted S.S. Obersturmbann Fuehrer Hoess, the camp commander, would saunter into the compound with S.S. Hauptsturm Fuehrer Wirths, his chief medical officer. Often the commander's small eyes were red-streaked from drinking.

INSPECTION FORESHADOWED DOOM

Slowly the commander and the doctor would walk down the lines of broken men. The inspection over, the commander would bark an order. Then he and his aide would leave the compound. As the two men walked away some of the prisoners would glance fearfully toward a small hut near the gate. Some of them kept their eyes to the ground. They did not have long to wait.

While the prisoners waited their guards would pace up and down behind them. The little rubber truncheons were always ready to perk up a stumbling man.

Soon the door of the hut would open and S.S. Oberschar Fuehrer Klehr would step out into the morning sunlight. Sometimes there were traces of egg around his thick lips. Always he carried a glittering hypodermic syringe in his right hand and a pint bottle in his left.

When he came to the first prisoner he would stick the syringe into the bottle. Two guards would stand near him. The sun always glinted on the short barrels of their tommy guns. As Oberschar Klehr would withdraw the needle from the bottle, the two guards would prod forward the first man in the line. If he was strong

DR. KAREL SPERBER

enough, he would remove his coat and shirt. If he was weak, another guard who wore rubber gloves would rip the rags from his back and throw them into a small cart.

Oberschar Klehr seemed bored with his job but he always did it quickly and efficiently. In a few moments the corpse of his first victim would be flung into a waiting cart and trundled toward a line of smoke-blackened furnaces. By January, 1945, Oberschar Klehr had injected carbolic acid into the hearts of 30,000 prisoners. He was well thought of at Gestapo headquarters. He played the piano well, too.

Sometimes a prisoner would resist. The guards didn't like this because after dealing with stubborn prisoners truncheons had to be cleaned. Sometimes, small pieces from a Jewish brain would mar the black crispness of their Gestapo uniforms. Russian and Polish blood was just as hard to remove.

Welcome Home!

Canada Welcomes with Pride and Gratitude the Victorious Men and Women of Her Armed Forces.

Well Done and Welcome Back

―――――――――

T. EATON C° LIMITED
OF MONTREAL

CHAPTER THIRTY

RECONVERSION

Post-war life did not suddenly return to normal, as Bob and I had so naively assumed it would that morning in the boat on VJ Day.

While it was true that gas rationing in Canada and the U.S. ended on VJ Day, other rationing and shortages continued as before.

In August, Cath told me with excitement, "Nylon stockings are supposed to be back by Christmas. I saw it in the paper."

"Super!" I said. We were easily pleased.

Bob was equally thrilled to read that month that the Ford Motor company had rolled its first 1946 model civilian passenger car off the assembly line, and hastened to his Ford dealer to have his name put on a waiting list. He was told that a 1946 version of the 1942 car wouldn't be available till the end of the summer of 1946 — a whole year away.

Then the salesman pointed out that the first customers eligible to buy new cars were doctors, nurses, ministers, and other people with priorities. For a dark moment it looked as if there may not be a Ford in Bob's future. I don't know what Bob said to indicate his impatience, but it made the car salesman say, "If you're going to take that attitude, Mr. Peate, we won't *sell* you a car." And Bob apologized. "And to think that during the Depression, car salesmen used to let my father take a car for a whole weekend to try it out," he said to me later.

The ads for the new Ford showed a group of women looking over a Ford Super Deluxe sedan, and saying things like, "I don't know synthetic enamel from a box of my children's paints...but if synthetic enamel is what it takes to make that beautiful, shiny, Ford finish, I'm all for it!" Another woman said, "My husband says the brakes are self-centering and hydraulic — whatever than means! All I know is they're so easy that I can taxi the children all day without tiring out!" Still another woman said, "Peter, he's my teen-age son, tells me that Ford is the only car in its price class with a choice of 100 horse-power V-8 engine or a brilliant new Six, that no matter which engine people pick, they're out front with Ford!" Still another woman claimed, "The interior of our Ford is strictly my department: "it's tailored with the dreamiest broadcloth. Such a perfect fit!" Another quote was, "Now here's another thing women like, and that's a blissfully comfortable ride — one that isn't bumpty-bump even on some of our completely forgotten roads."

Reading that ad made me wonder what had happened to the women who, mere months before, had been teaching men how to fly; handling explosives in munitions plants; testing the tensile strength of fabric to be used for parachute bags, tents, and uniforms; folding and packing parachutes; testing altimeters for planes; rivetting those planes; operating punch presses and lathes; teaching men how to assemble, adjust, and test-fire airplane machine guns; engraving instrument panels on planes; flying equipment and personnel; pouring TNT into shells; putting together hand grenades, land mines, and bombs; building aircraft; promoting boxing, delivering ice; training Ack-Ack gunners; farming; spotting aircraft; and, indeed, breaking up uranium atoms, in order to help make the atomic bomb.

Getting used to normalcy wasn't easy.

It was hard, for instance, for the 30,000 Montreal War Workers (along with War Workers across the country) to suddenly go from earning high salaries to being laid off their jobs.

It was equally difficult to adjust to a return of items that had so long been in short supply. In Miami, for instance, a fresh supply of soap and soap powder stocked on grocery shelves caused a riot among housewives, with one woman leaping on top of a pile of soap boxes and shouting at the clerks, "Come and get me!"

Another news story told of British children arriving in England after five years of living in the United States, sorry to have to leave the

194

U.S., and reluctant to be returning to their former homes where rationing and shortages were far worse than here.

When I read that, I wondered how the two sisters who had been in my class back in grammar school had felt about going back.

All through the war years a soap opera called "Soldier's Wife" had been running on the CBC, sponsored by the Wartime Prices and Trade Board. It covered the day-to-day life of a woman, Carry Murdock, whose soldier husband, George, was overseas.

The show's announcer introduced the program with the ponderous words, "Soldier's Wife — the story of Carry Murdock — a Canadian housewife — facing life — and its wartime problems — at home — in Canada."

"Aren't we all?" my mother asked the announcer each time he said it.

Besides showing how Carry carried on in her family life, the program's "commercial" breaks told its listeners how to cope with all the new rules and regulations the WPTB were handing us.

Once the war was over, the show was renamed "George's Wife" because Coping Carry's husband had returned home. The show remained on the air because The Wartime Prices and Trade Board's work was far from over. It still had to keep us informed on all the new Government agencies and Acts.

And, just as in wartime there had been a whole new vocabulary to get used to, so too in the postwar period were we exposed to a rash of new words.

If they had enough "points" to be discharged, "repatriates", (a.k.a. "repats") after "mustering out" received their "disembarkation pay"; plus their "demobilization" clothing allowance of a hundred dollars, with which they bought "priority suits" which were sold only on "Priority Certificates", to wear while applying for their "Re-Establishment Credits" while being "rehabilitated" during "reconversion". Dig?

By mid-October, war brides awaiting transport to Canada were increasing at the rate of 2,000 a month, but when they arrived they would find North America in the throes of the worst housing shortage in history. There was just no place for "man, woman, chicken, or chile", as singer Alberta Hunter would have put it.

The housing shortage was topic number one in every conversation. Jokes, cartoons, magazine ads and stories, as well as radio comedy skits dealt with the subject. It was the theme of movie comedies like "The More The Merrier" with Jean Arthur and Joel McCrea; and it was the inspiration for Charlie Barnet's record, "No Pad To Be Had", sung by the Delta Rhythm Boys.

Unscrupulous landlords were forcing returning vets to pay $600 for the key to their grungy apartments, demanding three months rent in advance, and making them buy shoddy, tacky second-hand furniture worth no more than $200 new for as much as $1,200.

Each ad for an apartment or flat to rent had some catch to it. Either the tenant would have to perform janitorial services, or the bathroom would be out in the hall and have to be shared by all the tenants on one floor. In other words, the apartment fit Wooly's definition of "uncanny".

Entire families were living in drafty, empty stores.

As the streetcar travelled along Ste. Antoine Street, on my way to work I saw little kids sitting in store windows, as if they were for sale.

My brother Choate was at the Canadian Repatriation Draft Camp at Nijmegen, Holland, on the German border, not eligible himself to return home yet, as he had arrived overseas in 1944, but working at facilitating the return of thousands of servicemen.

He had sent me a post card dated August 14th, 1945, and hadn't even mentioned the war being over. Perhaps because it wasn't yet over for him.

As he was an accountant, he had the prosaic job of working on the Army's books. He described what he did in a letter I received in September of 1945:

"I've been very busy since coming to this new camp. First I had to straighten out the mess, then set up a brand new system bringing everything up to date, close the books at the end of the month, make the financial statements, and show the auditors how to audit them before scramming on my ten day leave to Paris."

The most popular fashion item, though unobtrusive, was the General Service badge worn by returning veterans.

Larry, the boy with whom Wooly had been corresponding throughout the war, came home with one foot missing. Kenny C., the boy on the next street on whom I'd had the long-distance crush, never returned. The brother of the girl who lived up the street from him, whose front steps I sat on in order to feast my eyes on Kenny C., came back from the Merchant Marines a drug addict. He was sent directly to the new mental infirmary at Ste. Anne de Bellevue, where he would remain for the rest of his life. He had been a quiet, well-mannered boy of 17 when he signed up with the Merchant Marines.

196

Mitt's sister was mustered out of the CWACs, engaged to be married; Mitt's brother returned from the Navy in good shape, as did Wooly's brother, the Captain. We were fortunate indeed that no one in our immediately families had been killed or maimed in the war.

Kenny, the sailor with whom Mitt had corresponded, arrived home intact, but not to Mitt's welcoming arms. After he was safely back in circulation, she dumped him, despairing of his unromantic nature.

After a succession of letters from him that closed with such endearments as "Yours till the permanent waves"; "Yours till the Tootsie rolls"; and "Yours till Niagara Falls", she received a Valentine from him that read:

> Oh sweetheart mine
> with eyes divine
> will you be my Valentine?

She was so thrilled that old Kenny had finally come through in the romance department, that she produced the telegram at our next hen party, and read it aloud. After she read the first line, Wooly joined in and they recited it in unison.

When Mitt turned to look at Wooly in astonishment, Wooly picked up a telegraph envelope that was on top of the radio. "Larry sent me one too," she said.

"But how can that *be*?" Mitt said.

"The telegraph companies," Wooly told her, "have form telegrams for different occasions. All a serviceman has to do, is order the message he wants to send by number."

"By *number*?" Mitt repeated, "By *number*?" You mean Kenny *didn't* make up that poem all by himself?"

"I guess not."

"That does it. I'm going to give that unsentimental drip the brush off as soon as he gets back."

"Aw give the big lug another chance" Wooly urged, à la heroine's best friend in the movies.

But such a lack of personal involvement just wouldn't do for Mitt, who was so sentimental that I could clearly remember her becoming misty-eyed at the ribbon-cutting ceremony at the opening of the Kent Theatre.

At the same hen party, Cath brought out a letter from Alan, who was also in the Navy.

"He says he loves me," she said, looking chagrined.

"What's wrong with that?" Mitt asked.

"But I think he's icky," Cath said.

Gosh, what disparity. He loves her, and she thinks he's icky.

"What gave him the courage to tell you, then?" Wooly asked, "He must have thought you felt the same way."

"I don't know. I was just being polite in my letters. I never led him to believe I really liked him, as far as I know."

"Maybe it's just that he's been away so long," Mitt said, "and hasn't had a chance to meet any other girls."

"I don't know," said Cath, "but I always imagined that when a boy told me he loved me, that I'd be thrilled but it just made me feel jerky. I'll keep writing to him. but in a sisterly way. Maybe he'll get the message."

*

On the last day of 1945, the Canadian Press compiled a calendar of important dates of that year, calling it the most eventful year in history.

Seeing all the major events of the year set out month by month was chilling. The numbers of war casualties and deaths had a numbing effect.

Out of a population of less than 12 million souls, Canada suffered 103,000 war casualties and over 42,000 deaths. Quite apart from battle dead an estimated twelve million souls had been murdered by the Gestapo, the SS and the keepers of Nazi concentration camps. More than half of these innocent victims had been Jews and Poles.

Over 100,000 people were seared to death in Hiroshima, another 23,000 at Nagasaki. Within a few days, thousands who were not touched by the initial blasts died from radio active rays created by the explosions.

Literally millions of human beings, both friend and foe had been killed in the war. There had been indescribable pain and irreparable loss. Some survivers were doomed to a living death.

To what purpose? What were the gains? What would be better in the world now that that particular war had been fought? One third of my life had been lived in wartime, and I didn't understand the purpose of war any better when it was 'won' than when it started. But for those of us who lived through it, whether at home or away, wounded or whole, it would be a part of our collective consciousness, a frame of reference to help us recognize each other, even if the mark it left on us was invisible.

Indeed, the Canadian press could well have termed all six war years the most eventful in history. Those six years paralleled six of the most formative of our lives, and for us girls in our Sloppy Joe sweaters, wartime had come to be the norm. We had managed to adjust to it and regard it as a way of life. Now we were about to embark on the first peaceful year since it all began.

The "tumult and the shouting" of the victory celebrations died. The "captains and the kings" departed, to be replaced by young men in civilian clothes, not dashing uniforms. The element of danger and uncertainty ahead, that had put such a fine edge on the present, no longer threatened. And we were discovering that peacetime was taking as much getting used to as war.

1946—When Things Will Be Coming Our Way

Tomorrow a new year dawns—the first peaceful New Year in six long years of waiting and hoping. And with happier days ahead, we are dreaming of Things to Come. Slowly the swords are being turned into ploughshares—the guns and tanks and planes are being replaced on the assembly lines of the nation's huge factories with cars and radios and electric refrigerators. They may not all come in 1946; it takes time to work up to production great enough to supply a whole country denuded by six years of war. But one of these days reconversion will be completed and production will bring realization of the war-years' dream of a new washing machine, a new refrigerator, car, bicycle, camera and whatnot—including Nylons!

Courtesy of *The Gazette*, Montreal

EPILOGUE

I wrote my memories of this time with Emerson's words in mind: "That what is true for your private heart is true for others."

We grew up in an era that carried the official slogan: "Use it up, wear it out, make it do, or do without". Perhaps that accounts for our long-lasting loyalties.

The Sloppy Joe sweater stayed in fashion until 1947, when Christian Dior's "New Look" was introduced.

The music of that time — swing and jazz — lives on. The songs we sang have become standards. The films we watched are considered classics. The words and phrases of our "jive talk" are part of the vernacular. Our clothing fashions reappear cyclically; and we still seek out Sinatra's concerts and recordings.

Bob Peate and I married while I was still in my teens, but just before I went Lohengrinning down the aisle, I thought I saw, through my veil, the hazy figure of Joel McCrea, trench-coated, portable typewriter case in hand, snapping me a well-wishing salute, before disappearing forever into the London fog. Or perhaps that was just a Tulle Illusion.

Though I never became a foreign correspondent, I have enjoyed a long career in writing and broadcasting with the Canadian Broadcasting Corporation, and a newspaper in Los Angeles.

We girls in Sloppy Joe sweaters are grandmothers now, but because we grew up during the Second World War, and were "the girls they left behind them", we are members of an exclusive sorority:

Our song: "You'd Be So Nice To Come Home To"

Our sign: a V — for Victory

Our coat of arms: Quarterly — 1st, a telephone; 2nd, a Sinatra record; 3rd, knitting needles and wool; 4th Air Mail letters; the whole encircled with a string of pearls.

Our motto: Amor patitur moras.

M.P.
September 1989.